PRAISE F
THE UNFAIR AD

"God does not waste the experiences we go through . . . the good and the unpleasant. Aaron Burke uses his insight from Scripture and combines that with his life experiences to remind us that every setback and hurt can be used by God for our advantage! It will be to your advantage to read *The Unfair Advantage*."
—DOUG CLAY, GENERAL SUPERINTENDENT OF THE ASSEMBLIES OF GOD

"*The Unfair Advantage* is more than a book; it's a secret weapon, not only for turning pain into gain but turning disadvantages into opportunities! Aaron Burke is a master storyteller who has a way of making profound ideas accessible, relatable, and practical. This book is more than a good read; it's a gift that can change your life."
—DANIEL KOLENDA, PRESIDENT OF CHRIST FOR ALL NATIONS

"Aaron's not only a leader worth following and a speaker worth hearing but now an author worth reading. In *The Unfair Advantage* he profoundly paints the picture—utilizing the Bible character Joseph—that life's seemingly unfair obstacles are also opportunities to realize our greater purpose. We all find ourselves in darkroom seasons wanting to hurry our own development; this book equips us to wait expectantly, knowing there's potential in the process."
—JEFFERY PORTMANN, DIRECTOR OF CHURCH MULTIPLICATION NETWORK

"We have all faced unfair situations in our lives—moments that seemed to have no purpose or meaning. In his book, *The Unfair Advantage*, Aaron helps us see these experiences can be leveraged for our gain. With biblical insights and practical steps, this book will empower you to take advantage of the short end of the stick."
—DANIEL FLOYD, FOUNDING AND SENIOR PASTOR OF LIFEPOINT CHURCH

THE UNFAIR ADVANTAGE

THE
UNFAIR
ADVANTAGE

7 KEYS FROM THE LIFE OF JOSEPH FOR TRANSFORMING ANY OBSTACLE INTO AN OPPORTUNITY

AARON BURKE

NELSON
BOOKS

An Imprint of Thomas Nelson

Published in Nashville, Tennessee, by Nelson Books, an imprint of Thomas Nelson. Nelson Books and Thomas Nelson are registered trademarks of HarperCollins Christian Publishing, Inc.

Author is represented by The Fedd Agency, Inc., P. O. Box 341973, Austin, Texas 78734 with respect to the literary work.

Thomas Nelson titles may be purchased in bulk for educational, business, fundraising, or sales promotional use. For information, please email SpecialMarkets@ThomasNelson.com.

ISBN 978-1-4002-4324-2 (TP)
ISBN 978-1-4002-4325-9 (ePub)

Library of Congress Control Number: 2023005314

Printed in the United States of America

23 24 25 26 27 LBC 5 4 3 2 1

Dedicated to my bride, Katie Burke. You are one of my unfair advantages. We are better together, and I am forever grateful for you.

CONTENTS

Foreword by Mark Batterson xi

Introduction xv

Unfair Advantage #1: The Discouraged Dreamer 1

Unfair Advantage #2: The Redirected Reject 29

Unfair Advantage #3: The Wageless Worker 58

Unfair Advantage #4: The Seduced Saint 86

Unfair Advantage #5: The Oppressed Opportunist 115

Unfair Advantage #6: The Forgotten Faithful 135

Unfair Advantage #7: The Limited Leader 157

Conclusion: Discovering Your Unfair Advantage 181

Acknowledgments 197

Notes 199

About the Author 206

FOREWORD

BY MARK BATTERSON

"Life is unfair, then we die."

You've probably heard the expression.

You've probably felt it too.

When we find ourselves in situations we cannot control or comprehend, we ask questions like *Why me?* We second-guess ourselves, and we second-guess God. We even become passive-aggressive with God, like Mary and Martha. When Lazarus died, they each said to Jesus, "If you had been here, my brother would not have died." In other words, *it's not your fault, but it is, but it isn't, but it is.* Most of us have been there, asking God, *Where were you when I needed you?* But the reality is that God is right here. He's present in the normal ups and downs of your everyday life. He's there in the midst of the challenges you face. And if you take a learning posture, you will discover lessons you can leverage for the rest of your life. This book will help you do just that!

I have two rules of life that help me navigate unfair circumstances. One, when things go bad, don't play the victim.

Two, when things go good, don't play God. In my experience, there is fine a line between them. But if you want to get better, not bitter, you have to walk that line. You can't allow your past, especially the pain, to dictate your future!

Life may be unfair, but God is good. What you perceive to be a disadvantage may be an advantage in disguise! In *The Unfair Advantage* my friend Aaron Burke explores the story of Joseph and the unfair advantage God was providing him through the many seasons of unfairness. As Aaron unpacks seven of the biggest advantages Joseph received and shares highlights from his own experiences, I hope you'll have the courage to dream God-sized dreams all over again.

The first time I heard Aaron preach this message, I knew it was a book. More than a message, it's Aaron's life message. There will be seasons when it seems like dreams turn into nightmares, hopes turn into hurts. But there is a God who doesn't give up on us. Let's not give up on God. We have to identify the unfairness, then we have to activate the advantage!

With wisdom and candor, Aaron breaks down the lie that the pain of your past is holding you back, replacing it with the truth that your pain can actually become your greatest advantage. God is calling you to dream big again, and Aaron provides the tools and encouragement to do it, reminding us that we are in control of our own actions and attitudes. Aaron encourages us to do what others won't—to cultivate a good work ethic and take initiative to ensure that our pain doesn't go to waste. God won't waste it if we take the initiative to activate it. Insightful stories and discussion questions unveil the truths in our lives God is pointing us toward, whether it's a long-forgotten dream or a new one we just can't shake. This book will encourage you to examine the rejection you've faced in life and ask hard questions to survey your heart and motivations.

Several years ago, my wife, Lora, was diagnosed with cancer. It was a sucker punch, but then she read a poem that posed a question that caused us to examine our perspective. The question was this: *what have you come to teach me?* That's a hard question to ask, but asking it is the only way we grow through the tough times we will undoubtedly face.

In *The Unfair Advantage* Aaron's deep understanding of Scripture and his own relationship with God will give an inside look at how you can transform your pain into something better. It will give you the encouragement you need to make it through the toughest seasons of life. Whether it's dealing with deferred dreams or the sting of rejection, this too shall pass. There is a God who gives "beauty for ashes, the oil of joy for mourning, the garment of praise for the spirit of heaviness" (Isa. 61:3 KJV). As you read this book, I'm trusting that God will redeem the pain and the shame, transforming the unfairness into an unfair advantage, just like he did for Joseph!

INTRODUCTION

"It's unfair."

These are the words that stuck in my mind as tears rolled down my face in a dimly lit hotel conference room. For an hour, our team spread throughout the space, each person in their own moment of prayer. Music played quietly in the background as I walked throughout the room, taking time to pray with each one individually. The atmosphere seemed so peaceful and almost ordinary as I went from one person to the next. And then I got to one young woman.

Honestly, I am not much of a crier. There have been huge moments in my life where tears probably should have come. But whether during the devastating loss of a relationship, the momentous births of my children, or even watching a Hallmark movie that's notorious for being a tearjerker, I can usually be counted on to stay dry-eyed. Because of this, I consider it a sure sign that God is moving in my heart in those rare moments when I am actually moved to tears. So, on this cold January morning, his presence was obvious as I began praying for this staff member and a sudden tidal wave of empathy flooded my heart. Tears came and nothing could possibly have held them back.

This woman had walked into the youth group I was pastoring a decade earlier after her parents, who were pastors in our city, had gone through a brutal and public divorce. When I met her, she was angry and battling burdens that were far too heavy for anyone, especially someone so young. As time went on, God did an immense work in her, and his call on her life became extremely evident. Now all these years later, in a different city and in a different church, she had become a crucial part of our staff. However, as I prayed for her on this morning, the impact of God's presence hit me along with the weight of brokenness she was still carrying. I sensed in this moment the hurdles she was constantly fighting against. Her fractured past, issues in her personal circumstances, and even being a woman had caused her to believe there were more hurdles in front of her than others faced. The things that seemed easy for most people just weren't easy for her.

My prayers shifted, and as I thought about all she had gone through, the only words that came through my tears were "It's unfair."

It's unfair that she had walked through those hurts.

It's unfair that she dealt with all those struggles.

It's unfair that she didn't have the same opportunities others had.

It's unfair.

I stood there consumed with the heaviness of it all, and once again I experienced the movement of God. As I cried out to him, "It's unfair," he whispered to me, "It is unfair, but it's to her advantage."

That was it. All of the trials, all of the struggles, and all of the setbacks were actually the unfair advantage God was setting up for her. These "obstacles" were preparing her for the opportunities only she would be able to accomplish.

This is the entire premise of this book. Many of us are stuck under the weight of an unfair circumstance. We may see it as that one thing holding us back from God's great purpose for our lives. But what if . . .

Adversity is my greatest advantage.
Struggle is a setup for a bigger stage.
Man's rejection is many times God's direction.
Obstacles are simply opportunities in disguise.
What was "intended to harm me . . . God intended it
    for good" (Gen. 50:20).

If you have spent a fair amount of time in church, you have probably heard these statements before. They are great preaching points. They are inspirational. They can get a crowd excited. But when the adversity or rejection or struggle becomes a real-life thing, it can be hard to remember these truths.

The young woman from my church, as well as so many of us, may have believed that our problem has left us limited, our dream is out of reach, and our future is not what it could have been. But what we often don't realize is that those deficits are the things God can use to shape our destiny.

The key word is "can." Just because something negative happened to you doesn't mean you are leveraging it for your ultimate purpose. This book will give you the keys to turning something unfair into something that is for your advantage. I worked for two years researching through the scriptures and gathering life experiences of exactly how God "causes everything to work together for the good" (Rom. 8:28 NLT).

AVAILABLE . . . BUT NOT AUTOMATIC

There is a lie that must be addressed in the opening pages of this book. It is a lie communicated through self-help books and even behind pulpits in churches. The lie sounds something like this: "it *will* be used for good." All the pain, all the rejection, all the struggle is actually helping us move toward our destiny. These words are comforting, but they aren't necessarily true. Just because something bad happened to you doesn't mean it will position you to receive something good from it. It is available, but it is not automatic.

I am a sucker for travel-loyalty programs. A few years back I reached "Diamond" status in a hotel chain because of the ridiculous number of nights I'd stayed in their hotel over the previous year. I was proud of this accomplishment that I thought meant I got a reserved parking spot closer to the lobby and a later checkout time than everyone else.

Six months after achieving Diamond status, I was checking into one of their hotels near Disney World in Orlando. As I was talking to the lady at the front counter, she asked me if I ever got an upgrade. I responded with "I didn't know upgrades were available." She explained how upgrades are almost always available, but they aren't automatic. You must request it. I submitted my request that night and got bumped into the Presidential suite. I was shocked. This had been available the entire time, but I had no clue; it was available but not automatic.

This is how your unfair scenarios work. There is an upgrade to your pain and struggle. But it won't come automatically. There are things you need to do, attitudes you need to adopt, resolve you need to gain, and effort you have to put in to walk into your destiny.

This book will walk you through the strategy required to turn what is negative into what is necessary for your destiny to come to pass. You will be challenged. You will be encouraged. You will be stretched.

If your past has been hard, this book is for you.

If you feel like you have been shortchanged, this book is for you.

If you feel discouraged because of a setback, this book is for you.

If you are looking for hope in a current struggle, this book is for you.

Buckle in—maybe, just maybe, everything that is unfair is really for your advantage.

THINGS ARE NOT AS THEY SHOULD BE

God does not cause our pain, but he can use our pain for a greater purpose. This statement is inspirational, but it is rooted in a deep theology of how God operates in the world today. The psalmist wrote, "The highest heavens belong to the

Lord, but the earth he has given to mankind" (Ps. 115:16). God has turned over this earth to mankind, but we haven't done the best job at taking care of it.

The result of sin in our world today is that things are not as they should be. Our world is broken. A hot and gooey Krispy Kreme donut is 170 calories, yet a piece of celery is 15 calories. This is very unfair! Why is everything that tastes good bad for you, yet everything that tastes bad is good for you? Don't tell me you crave healthy food. That isn't normal. I crave cookie dough ice cream at 10 p.m. *That* is normal.

Life became complicated when sin entered the world at the fall of Adam and Eve. God's good creation became twisted and broken. In Genesis 3, we read some of the consequences of the impact of sin. I have watched my wife give birth to five children—the pain in childbirth is no joke!

What we see on earth is not God's will. In the last couple of years, the impact of sin has been significantly experienced at a worldwide level. Based on conservative projections, over six million people have perished because of the COVID-19 pandemic. With the spread of illness, mandatory lockdowns, masks, and social distancing, it appears no one on our globe has been unaffected by the impact of this pandemic.

In the United States alone, we have faced a health crisis, a mental health crisis, a financial crisis, a racial crisis, and political turmoil all in one year's time. Experts believe that over 160 million people (many of them women and children) are on the verge of starvation, and because of the financial crisis, relief organizations are cutting their budgets instead of expanding them to meet the demand.[1] This is a solid example of how broken our world is and how fragile life is. This couldn't have been God's plan.

When Jesus was teaching his disciples how to pray, he asked his Father, "May your will be done on earth, as it is in heaven" (Matt. 6:10 NLT). God's will is perfectly accomplished in heaven. It is a place with "no more death or mourning or crying or pain" (Rev. 21:4). What a beautiful thought! And this is God's desire for mankind. Jesus challenges us to pray for his will to be done on earth.

So what is God's response to suffering and heartache? We can answer this by considering his response as he walked on earth two thousand years ago. Paul wrote to the church at Colossae, "For in Christ all the fullness of the Deity lives in bodily form" (Col. 2:9). We know the character of God because we can study the life of Christ.

Through the biblical narrative we find that Jesus had a two-pronged approach to the problems he encountered. Whenever he approached pain, Jesus' response was either to *change it* or to *use it*. People mistakenly get angry at God because they do not understand this.

Throughout the Gospels there are many powerful stories of Jesus changing a situation. Matthew 9:35 says, "Jesus went through all the towns and villages, teaching in their synagogues, proclaiming the good news of the kingdom and healing every disease and sickness." Blind eyes were opened, the dead raised, children cured, demon-possessed men set free. The impossible becomes possible when Jesus gets involved.

For some reason beyond my understanding, Jesus will

also sometimes choose a second response to hardship. There are times when he doesn't heal the infirmity or prevent the pain. Take, for example, his cousin, John the Baptist. Jesus' words in Matthew 11:11 were "Truly I tell you, among those born of women there has not risen anyone greater than John the Baptist." Yet Scripture tells us that John was imprisoned and finally beheaded. Jesus did not stop John's death, but he certainly used John's life. In Acts 18, John's influence in preaching Christ was still seen decades after his life on earth had ended.

When God doesn't solve our hurt, he spins it for a greater purpose. Solve it or spin it, those are the two options with God. Be encouraged. If you are going *through* something, it is *for* something. Paul reinforced the nature of God when he wrote, "And we know that in all things God works for the good of those who love him, who have been called according to his purpose" (Rom. 8:28). If you are frustrated because your situation wasn't resolved, it may be that God is redirecting your situation. He can solve it, or he can spin it for a greater purpose.

> If you are going *through* something, it is *for* something.

NOTHING IS WASTED WITH GOD

Moses may have thought his life was nearing the end at eighty years old. Time for retirement. He had spent the past forty years as a shepherd in the desert, working for his father-in-law, Jethro. It could be that Moses viewed these years as an escape from the baggage of his past in Egypt. However, he soon discovered that rather than only running *from* something, God had him also running *for* something. He may not have realized it at the time, but all those years of learning how to herd sheep would equip him with the skills needed to herd thousands of people through a wilderness. A time that could have been dismissed as pointless actually became a time of intense preparation. Waiting seasons are not wasted seasons with God. If you find yourself waiting, don't view it as God punishing you. Ask instead, could he be preparing you?

Every hurt, every loss, every pain, every setback, every letdown, and every season is uniquely designed by God to prepare you for what he has for you next. Moses first learned to move sheep, and then God promoted him to moving people. Lots of people! Some theologians believe it could have been between 1.5 and 2 million people that Moses ushered through the very desert he sat in for forty years as a shepherd. Moses was God's choice to deliver the Israelites not in spite of his history, but because of his history.

Developmental seasons are usually dark seasons. Beautiful pictures are developed in what photographers call the *darkroom*. It is the same with life. The developmental years are usually the dark seasons that could be described as overlooked, overanalyzed, overcomplicated, or overextended, but they are also overwhelmingly necessary for where you are going. If you short-circuit the process, you will eventually short-circuit the product.

Embrace every tough season with the expectation that this is a seed being planted toward an unknown yet unrivaled future. Years after Moses, we see in Scripture the story of the warrior-king, David. He is known for his courageous defeat of the giant Goliath. But before facing giants, he spent years facing bears and lions as he faithfully protected his sheep. David probably had no clue that those little moments would be foundational to his later role of protecting God's people and expanding God's kingdom. If Jesus hasn't yet answered your prayer, it may be he is using your pain to build your ultimate platform.

When something negative occurs, it is human nature to ask, "Why did this happen?" Jesus confronted this in John 9 when he was asked why a man was born blind. "Rabbi, who sinned, this man or his parents, that he was born blind?" (John 9:2).

"Neither . . ." Jesus answered. "This happened so that the works of God might be displayed in him" (John 9:3). Jesus completely shifted the perspective from "What made this happen?" to "What is the ultimate purpose?" This is our unfair advantage. Not everything will make sense here on earth. All will be made clear, however, one day in eternity.

UNDERSTANDING AN UNFAIR ADVANTAGE

The idea of an unfair advantage is often used in the sports world. I live in Tampa, and since our church launched in 2013, I admit to occasionally making jokes from the stage about how bad the Tampa Bay Buccaneers have played. In my defense, Tampa was one of the worst teams in the entire league. For years, the team's losses overwhelmingly exceeded any wins. In 2020, however, Tom Brady, the undisputed GOAT (greatest of all time) of American football, left the New England Patriots and signed a two-year, $30 million deal with the Bucs.[2] Brady is no average quarterback. Prior to Tampa, he had already achieved six Super Bowl victories, yet his critics refused to give him credit. They attributed these wins solely to the leadership within the New England Patriots. His haters were silenced, however, when Brady joined the Bucs and that same year took what had been the worst team in the NFL to a Super Bowl victory. This was the team's first Super Bowl in almost two decades and, incredibly, was the only time the host city was playing in the game. I am not a huge football fan, but even I knew how momentous this night was!

Having Tom Brady on your football team is an unfair advantage. I like to think Brady knew what kind of history he would make when he joined Tampa Bay. He gave a struggling team an unfair advantage and it won them a Super Bowl. The bad years leading up to the victory made this the kind of inspirational story that will be celebrated for years to come.

Another example is basketball. At six feet three, I am regularly asked if I play. I have absolutely no basketball skills, but because I am taller than average, people sometimes assume I must be really good. What most people don't realize is that even if I *did* have the talent, I am still too short to have a fighting chance at any kind of basketball career.

If you want to play in the NBA, you have about a one-in-a-million chance of making it. But if you are over seven feet tall, that changes to about a one-in-six chance of being in the NBA. Think about being seven feet tall. Your feet always hanging off the bed. Having difficulty finding a good pair of pants. Never able to be in the front of group pictures. That's unfair, right? But if you love sports and have some measure of athletic ability, your height affords you a prize opportunity that not many other people would ever be able to experience. That is the unfair advantage.

Let's look at how this concept plays into the business world. Amazon dominated the consumer industry during the COVID-19 pandemic based on an unfair advantage. For years, Amazon had been laying the groundwork for an entirely online shopping experience that would deliver products to your doorstep in record time. When the world shut down in March of 2020, Amazon was already a phenomenon—but in a year when other businesses experienced extreme setbacks, Amazon had its most profitable year on record, bringing in over $380 billion. Its stock soared 70 percent and founder Jeff Bezos reportedly grew his personal wealth by $75 billion.[3] How is that all possible? Well, it all comes down to its unfair advantage. It was the perfect storm for Amazon. No one could capitalize on the moment quite like it because it already had the infrastructure and technology in place to deal with the world's being stuck at home.

People may look with envy upon the person or team or company experiencing an unfair advantage. The truth, though, is while success may be easily seen, there may also be a fair amount of struggle hidden underneath. This book is not called The Advantage. The focus is not on your great talents or easy accomplishments but on the trials that pave the way for triumph.

SELLING AVOCADOS

My father exemplifies the principle of an unfair advantage. He was raised in a rough part of Miami during the 1960s and '70s. His father was a compulsive gambler, regularly using their family savings to feed his addiction. When he won, it was cause for a family celebration. The losses, however, were sadly far more frequent. Eventually my grandfather ended up gambling away everything, including my dad's college fund.

Many times while he was growing up, my dad would get home from school and there would be no food in the house because all their grocery money had been gambled away. It was unfair. One day, after discovering there was no food, my dad got desperate and decided to take matters into his own teenage hands.

His hungry stomach probably led him to make his next decision. He found some avocados growing abundantly in his area of Miami. Instead of eating them, though, he decided to fill up a bucket and head down to the local market. He stood on the street corner and went to work. In a matter of hours, my dad had sold his entire bucket of fruit for twenty-five cents apiece or five for a dollar. My dad should have been enjoying his junior high school years. Instead, a hungry young kid was forced to sell fruit on the side of the street. It was unfair, but little did he know it would work for his advantage.

Selling food on the side of the street in Miami is how my dad received his first bit of sales experience. He found the right words to say and the words to avoid. He learned the art of building rapport with his clients. My dad would often tell me later, "They will buy into *you* before they buy into your product." He went on to be the top salesman in his marketing company and then later opened multiple car businesses. The life he provided for me and my siblings was far beyond anything he received growing up. He is honestly a sales genius, and his foundational skills can be traced back to selling avocados as a teenager. Unfair? Yes. But it was for his advantage.

AN OVERNIGHT SUCCESS?

Apple founder Steve Jobs said, "If you really look closely, most overnight successes took a long time."[4] Greatness isn't made in a day, it is made daily. Think about all those success stories that seem so instant and easy. While we are in on the highlight reels, I would bet most of these stories are also full of behind-the-scenes disappointments and frustrations. Successful people haven't avoided failure, but they have used failure for a greater purpose.

Our tendency is to sweep our failures under the rug and to post our successes on social media. We hide the parts of our story that are sad and celebrate the parts that are victorious. This is a major mistake. People get the impression that it takes success to be successful. That is not true. It takes persistence to be successful. The world belongs not to the ultra-talented but to the ultra-stubborn person who won't quit.

When confronted with the large number of failed inventions in his life, Thomas Edison responded, "Why, man, I have gotten a lot of results! I know several thousand things that won't work."[5] I love this perspective! It is the heart behind understanding the unfair advantage. We refuse to look through a negative lens on our negative experiences. We only lose if we quit. Scripture reminds us, "Let us not become weary in doing good, for at the proper time we will reap a harvest if we do not give up" (Gal. 6:9).

We have two options when we look at the unfair areas of our lives: be a victim or be a visionary.

Victims are discouraged. Visionaries are determined.
Victims get embittered. Visionaries get empowered.
Victims only see problems. Visionaries see potential.
Victims quit. Visionaries pick up where the victims
    left off.
Victims see dirt. Visionaries see the gold in the midst
    of the dirt.
Victims are frustrated. Visionaries are fueled by
    potential.
Victims see the test. Visionaries see the testimony.

You can be a visionary. You can choose to look at your situation through a new lens.

So, let's identify the situation. What do you see as your setback? What is unfair?

Is it your upbringing?
Your education?
Your personality?
Your failures?
Your looks?
Your IQ?
Your relationship history?
Your struggles?

THE UNFAIR LIFE OF AARON

I know the unfair advantage well. School was never easy for me. Making friends never came naturally. Sports were just embarrassing since I have absolutely no talent for any of them. My dad, whom I love deeply and who is a great provider, also had a major drug problem all throughout my childhood and college years. I was expelled from a Christian high school (more on this later). While working on my degrees, I continually failed and had to retake courses. Our church started in a run-down dollar theater because not a single school wanted us to rent their facility. Oh, and I'm called to preach but I lose my voice almost every time I give a sermon. I hired a speech therapist for this a few years ago, and she basically told me I'm a lost cause! I say all of this just to let you know I also feel the pain of the unfair.

We live life forward, but we understand life backward.[6] This phrase has been revolutionary for my life. It wasn't until I intentionally looked backward on my life that I began to see every one of those unfair experiences was also a catalyst toward the impact God has made through me. I walk with greater compassion, humility, and dependence on God, simply because life hasn't been easy.

As I look back, I realize there were intentional choices I made at every unfair season or scenario that caused that event to work for my ultimate good. I could have sat back, but I leaned in and leveraged each event to move me toward my destiny. I faced lots of failures—you will read about them throughout this book—but I also had some big wins.

You can make the hard choice during hard times. Everything worthwhile is uphill. If it is difficult, it is worth doing. Culture has accustomed people to take the path of least resistance. Therefore, few achieve significance with their lives. Your salvation is free, only available through the gift of grace offered by Jesus on the cross, but your significance is costly. It is accessed only on a road called unfair. It is a journey that is worth taking.

THE UNFAIR LIFE OF JOSEPH

In this book we will look at seven different unfair advantages in the life of Joseph from the book of Genesis. Joseph had a crazy dream that was achieved through the most non-traditional and difficult path. In the end, he advanced to second-in-command over all of Egypt and was used to save his entire family. How did it happen? He capitalized on his unfair advantages. More on this later, but here is a little background on Joseph; you will need this information to make the most of the story you are going to hear throughout the rest of this book.

Joseph lived some seventeen hundred years before Jesus came to earth. Joseph was born to a powerful lineage. God had given his great-grandfather, Abraham, a special promise that his descendants would be God's chosen people. God reaffirmed this covenant with Joseph's grandfather, Isaac, and then his father, Jacob.

Joseph was the eleventh son born to Jacob. His name means "he adds" as in "he adds another son." I wonder if on the eleventh son, Jacob ran out of names and just decided to say, "Here's another one!" Not much is said about Joseph until he is seventeen years old. Genesis 37:2 says, "Joseph, a young man of seventeen, was tending the flocks with his brothers." In short, Joseph had a normal life doing normal tasks any teenager living in Canaan over thirty-seven hundred years ago would have done.

But then the Scriptures give us a little insight into the family dynamic—or I might say the family dysfunction. "Jacob loved Joseph more than any of his other children because Joseph had been born to him in his old age. So one day Jacob had a special gift made for Joseph—a beautiful robe" (Gen. 37:3 NLT). I couldn't imagine favoring one of my kids over another. But if I did, there is no way I would tell anyone about it! (If my kids are reading this in the future, I seriously didn't have favorites, at least not in 2022.) So Jacob let everyone in on the fact that Joseph was his favorite by giving him this special, ornate robe.

But the robe did not do what Jacob thought it would do. I always thought Joseph had an easy path toward success because his father favored him and blessed him with this robe. But the favor of his father and the special robe weren't to his advantage. The robe was really just a human attempt at an advantage.

In fact, when Joseph was forced to leave Canaan, the robe never made it out with him, and it was definitely *not* the tool that made him second-in-command over all of Egypt some thirteen years later. His advantage wasn't his family's reputation, or his father's favor, or his special coat. Success will not come from something handed to you, but from how you handle something difficult.

> Success will not come from something handed to you, but from how you handle something difficult.

This is your unfair advantage.

Let me say that again, because if you miss this, you miss the point of this book. Success will not come from something handed to you, but from how you handle something difficult.

From Genesis 37 to Genesis 50, Joseph went on a wild ride. He hit one unfair obstacle after another. For thirteen years, Joseph couldn't catch a break. Sound like the story of your life? Be encouraged. What was difficult ended up being defining. Joseph started with multiple disadvantages: a discouraging past that was filled with frustration, rejection by his brothers, a work environment where he was deeply undervalued, temptation and attempted seduction by his employer's wife, imprisonment for something he didn't do—this list goes on. Joseph's life was full of pain. But in the end, he arrived at his God-given purpose.

HOW TO READ THIS BOOK

In the chapters ahead, we're going to highlight these unfair scenarios from Joseph's life, many or all of which you'll identify with at some level. But those unfair scenarios will be combined with a challenge of how to turn that unfair scenario for your advantage. It might be painful, but it will be for a greater purpose. I am not writing this simply to inspire you but to *equip* you to see every unfair situation used for your advantage and for God's glory. To add to the practical takeaways, each chapter has discussion questions at the end. To get the fullest impact from the book, I encourage you to complete these assignments. Some of the best learning comes by doing, and I want to give you the tools to best learn.

Finally, this book is best read in community. I would encourage you to gather some friends and go through the seven lessons together. They will have insight and stories that can help solidify the lessons learned from the life of Joseph.

Be honest with your group. There might be parts of your story you are ashamed of. Normally the unfair areas of our lives are the parts we sweep under the rug and try not to think about ever again. This shouldn't be the case. These areas are crucial to your story and could be the very testimony needed to bring hope to someone else.

You might see your pain as a setback, a weakness, an obstacle, or a problem. My hope is that you soon begin to see how God can use these as a setup for something great. Embrace this journey. It might seem unfair, but let's discover how it is for your advantage.

THE DISCOURAGED DREAMER

Joseph had a dream, and when he told it to his brothers, they hated him all the more.

GENESIS 37:5

My favorite cartoon growing up was *Animaniacs*. The main characters were Disney-looking rip-offs named Yakko, Wakko, and their sister Dot. I was addicted to the show's dry yet very witty humor. Thanks to Hulu, which rebooted the cartoon after a twenty-year hiatus, my kids and I get to experience the new episodes together. We just laugh and laugh.

Each week the show has a segment that features two characters named Pinky and the Brain. Pinky is a ditzy, tall, and skinny mouse while the Brain is a short, big-headed, brilliant mouse who, like his name suggests, is "the brains" of the operation. Every episode is the same: the Brain comes up with a new strategy for world domination—and every episode it fails.

Each show ends the same way. After their failed global takeover, Pinky and the Brain find themselves back in their cage as laboratory mice. Pinky closes out each episode by walking up to the Brain and asking him, "What are we going to do tomorrow, Brain?" And the Brain responds in a villain-ous type of voice, "The same thing we do every day, Pinky. Try and take over the world."

This is the key to living the life of the unfair advantage. When the dream fails, you determine to dream again. Every day is a new day to conquer the world. Every day we are given another opportunity to see lives changed. Every day God's mercies are new. Every day we get a fresh start at a lasting success. Every day dreamers see the potential for their moment of breakthrough.

The Brain is the eternal optimist. He failed one day, but he will try again the next. Our expectations for what *could be* must not be based on the experiences of what *has been*. No one can move forward while looking backward. That's sure to lead to a massive crash. No matter how you may have fallen before, get up and keep walking. According to a quote commonly ascribed to Malcolm Forbes, "When you cease to dream, you cease to live."

DREAM BIG

God believes in you. The question is, do *you*? When is the last time you truly dreamed big? When is the last time you got alone with him and thought, *What could God do through me?* I have found my greatest dreams do not come through my own strategizing but through the Spirit. God desires more than anyone that none should perish, and he has a dream for world domination (2 Peter 3:9). What is your part in this? As the saying goes, "The future belongs to those who believe in the beauty of their dreams." Those who do big things are usually the ones who dreamed big things. Everything significant starts with a dream, and every dream makes its home in the heart of a dreamer. It is time to dream again.

I can picture Joseph staring up at the clouds and imagining what life would be like one day, pondering what his future could hold. In the life of a dreamer, there is a unique dissatisfaction for what the world has already offered them. The status quo is not okay. What quenches the desires of culture doesn't quench the desires of dreamers.

One early morning when I was sixteen years old, I had a God moment on a hillside in Nepal. I will never forget sitting outside of a rustic hotel overlooking the Himalayan mountains as the sun was rising. Directly in front of me was Annapurna I, the tenth-highest mountain in the world, also known to be the deadliest for all mountain climbers. Sitting so small beneath it, I was in awe of its massive size. It was majestic. While staring at this mountain, I was overcome by how big God is.

Awestruck in the presence of God's magnitude and power, I had a sudden realization of how small all my goals had been. None of my plans so far could measure even close to his miraculous nature. I had to start dreaming big. We dream big because our God is big. When we get a glimpse of the invisible, we are able to dream about the impossible. Show me the size of your goals, and I will show you the size of your God.

My life was changed on the side of that hill in Pokhara, Nepal. As the saying goes, "The two most important days in your life are the day you are born and the day you find out why." This moment marked my discovery of why I exist, and I made a commitment that I would use my life for God's call. He instilled in me this determination to make my life count. Without delay I began to strategize how he could use me to change the world. In other words, I became a dreamer.

Coming home from that summer mission trip was tough. I had experienced a glimpse of the greatness of God, and I didn't want to return to the mundane life. Nevertheless, a few weeks into my return, I found myself once again back in the routine of eleventh grade. That pivotal message from Nepal was still taking root, however, and one day while daydreaming in history class, it once again tried to break free. I was staring out the window, halfway listening to the teacher's lecture, when a random thought popped into my head: *I don't want to learn history. I want to make it.* This wasn't a desire for worldly fame. This was a desperation for godly purpose.

Your story may be similar. Maybe you dream of what

could be instead of what is. Embrace this dreamer side! Begin to focus on the future instead of all the failures. View things in light of your legacy rather than your limitations. See what no one else sees so that you can do what no one else will do. Some may call you foolish; I call it being a dreamer.

The world is changed by people who have grasped the right combination of dreaming and doing. If you are going to start down any path of significance, you have to learn to be okay when people misunderstand your dreams and intentions.

My kids are dreamers. They are always telling me big dreams of one day being astronauts, vets, or scientists. My daughter recently told me that when she grows up, she wants to be an artist. I am her biggest fan, but I have seen her artwork, and let's just say it is special only to me and her mother. I love that she is too young to base her dream on anything other than this great potential she sees herself capable of. I want to live my life with this kind of childlike faith.

What is the dream in your heart? What keeps you up at night? What makes you come alive when you talk about it? I often meet people who dream of planting churches, opening businesses, eradicating sex trafficking, ending abortion, revolutionizing the foster care system, translating the Bible, funding the expansion of the gospel, and countless other crazy, big ideas. As they share their dreams, I also frequently hear the question, "Do you think this is something God wants me to do?" My response is always the same: "Where do you think these dreams are from?" Dreaming big is not the norm. Settling for what is safe is. Our God-given destiny starts with a God-given dream. Remember, if it's too big for you, it is the perfect size for God.

BEING MISUNDERSTOOD

It is painful to be misunderstood. When Katie and I were engaged, we were living a long distance from each other. She was in her last semester of nursing school and called me one week to tell me that she had passed her final nursing exam. She then asked if I was going to be able to drive the seven-hour trip to her pinning ceremony. I was excited for her and congratulated her on finishing, but I let her know I wouldn't be able to make it since Wednesdays were youth ministry nights for me.

In my defense, I had never heard of a pinning ceremony. Katie calmly said, "That's fine," and in my naive, unmarried mind I thought that was the end of the conversation. Since then, I have come to learn "that's fine" does not mean "that's fine." What it actually means is "everything is the furthest from fine." I found out later that Katie almost ended our engagement that night. I misunderstood the importance of the event, and she misunderstood my level of commitment to her based on my bad decision. Thankfully we were able to work things out, and I have learned a lot since then!

Although our situation is unique, misunderstandings happen to everyone. They are responsible for all sorts of conflict in every type of relationship. They are also common obstacles world changers face when describing their big dreams to others.

For example, the book of Genesis gives us the account of two dreams Joseph had. In both of the dreams, he saw himself in a place of power over his family. He told his ten older brothers, in Genesis 37:7, "We were binding sheaves of grain out in the field when suddenly my sheaf rose and stood upright, while your sheaves gathered around mine and bowed down to it." (I wonder if every eleventh child has dreams like this?)

Joseph's brothers were ticked and immediately began judging his motives. They said, "Do you intend to reign over us? Will you actually rule us?" Their assumptions were like poison and "they hated him all the more because of his dream and what he had said" (Gen. 37:8). Just as in Joseph's case, there are many times when those closest to you are the last people to believe in you. Why is this? One reason could be because these are the people who know your pattern. They are busy judging you based on your past. God, on the other hand, is looking at your potential.

Pattern is what you have done. *Potential* is what is possible. Our God-given dreams are easily misunderstood by those closest to us because others see only our pattern as the predictor of our future. God sees things differently. God knows our patterns but still promises us incredible potential.

Based on Joseph's pattern, his life should have been to continue the family business as a shepherd, and as the eleventh in line, he would be subordinate to each of his older brothers. That was the pattern, but his potential was based

> We are no longer what people think we are; we are who God says we are.

on God's specific task for him that was bigger than he could have imagined. Like Joseph's, your pattern might be wrapped up in your family history. But as a believer in Jesus Christ, your potential comes alive based on a greater family history, the family of God. We are no longer what people think we are; we are who God says we are.

If you are going to start down any path of significance, you have to learn to be okay when people misunderstand your dreams and intentions. Joseph's brothers believed he was dreaming about them worshiping him. They were irate at what they thought they understood. Because we see the end of the story, we know Joseph's dream was truly about him saving his family's lives.

In God's view, prominence is not given for the purpose of honor. It is for the purpose of helping. Leadership should not be pursued to be better seen. It should be used to be a better servant. When you dream of greatness, get ready for people to challenge you instead of cheer you on. People who do not grow are usually critics of those who do.

DEALING WITH CRITICISM

When a dream from God grips your heart, it will eventually consume your life. For Joseph, he couldn't keep his mouth shut. He shared his dreams with his brothers, igniting their wrath and ridicule in response. Voicing everything to everyone was a mistake. Not all that God tells you is for everyone around you. I know this firsthand. When I was a young adult, full of excitement over all that God was doing in me, I shared with everyone I knew my dreams of traveling the world and telling people about Jesus. To my disappointment, instead of support, I had multiple family members tell me to get a "real degree" so I could get a "real job."

What voice are you going to believe? The strongest and most consistent voice we listen to will always win. So, in a crucial season of my life, I questioned everything God had spoken to me because of a family member's insistence I should pursue a different degree in college. Although the pressure was real, I knew what I was called to.

The ordinary person will not understand those with extraordinary dreams. In placing such high value on what is comfortable and familiar, people lose the capacity to dream further than what is normal. It is rumored that Henry Ford never asked people for their opinion of his Model T vehicle. As Adam Hartung wrote, "It may be apocryphal, but Henry Ford supposedly said, 'If I had asked my customers what they wanted, they would have told me a faster horse.'"[1]

The world is full of critics who have settled for far less than God's best for their lives. Many times, these are the people whose opinions are the loudest when they see other people stepping out to accomplish something big. As dreamers begin to share their hearts, out of the critic's mouth comes only negativity and critique. This is unfair. It's unfair that criticism and not celebration are common responses. It's unfair that people don't champion each other in the times when support is needed most. It's unfair when we don't believe in each other as much as God does.

Big dreams come with big criticism. Often the criticism starts with unfair judgment:

- "You just want attention."
- "You need to get a real job."
- "Your head is always in the clouds."
- "Get back to reality."
- "Who are you to think you can make a difference?"

An attack of criticism creates a battle in the mind. It is harmless to simply hear a lie, but it is destructive to believe one. Where the mind goes, the man follows. The Enemy is working overtime on disqualifying what God has qualified. Criticism is a tactic he will use to carry out his sinister plans.

I wonder if Joseph longed for the approval of his brothers in the same way we all crave the approval of the people in our lives. It's a struggle that most of us face. Eventually, however, the decision must be made. Will I live based on the opinion of a limited man or instead choose to follow the plan of a limitless God? Galatians 1:10 drives this point home in saying, "If I were still trying to please people, I would not be a servant of Christ." So stand firm and let me ask you again: Whose voice will you believe?

I am so thankful for people like my mom. When so many others proved to be critics, she was my dream champion. She never judged my intentions or told me my goals were out of reach. And if she ever did think those things, I would never have known it. She was always one of my biggest fans.

One of the scariest days of my life was in November 2012, when I officially quit my job to move to Tampa, with nothing but my family and a dream of starting a church. My wife was quitting her job as well. That moment when I received my last paycheck was terrifying. Now I had no income to raise funds for a church, move to a new town, or feed my family without complete and total reliance on God.

My first day of unemployment, my mom asked me to meet her for breakfast before our big move. I walked into that small breakfast café with so much stress, and I spent the next hour venting it all out. I shared all of my fears of failing. I shared all of my doubts. I was completely vulnerable as I shared all aspects of my dream with my mom, and as she listened, she also spoke life. She spoke life over me and how much she believed in me and in Katie. She spoke life over our church and encouraged me in what I knew God had said. And then she reached into her purse and pulled out a check she had written for $500. It was the first check I had seen made out to Radiant Church. That tangible sight, at such a crucial time, made me cry like a baby. Someone believed in me and was willing to invest in my dream. I am moved every time I think of this act that not only encouraged me in the moment but also stirred my faith that God would continue to provide.

It is unfair that more of our family and friends don't champion our dreams like my mom did. To the best of our knowledge, no one in Joseph's family believed in his dream. But God did. Even if no one else stands beside you, always remember God is in your corner. You might be criticized by man, but you are championed by God.

WHOM WILL YOU BELIEVE?

A God-given dream is a desire so big that it couldn't possibly be accomplished without God. That quest can be achieved only through faith and a miracle. It could be an improbable business idea, a hopeful prayer for a specific relationship, or a call to ministry with more questions than answers. Whatever it is, be encouraged. Again, if it's too big for you, it is the perfect size for God.

How do we know if a dream is from God? Sometimes differentiating between a man-made idea and a God-breathed truth is easy. Other times, determining the source of a dream seems a little more vague. This is such an important distinction to make because if it is a *God* dream, then it's worth giving everything to reach it. If, however, it's only a *good* dream, then spending any time and energy in chasing it could be futile.

As we spend time praying for God's will and direction, Scripture is the perfect place to hear his voice. Romans 12:1–2 has always been my go-to passage when I am searching for God's will in my life: "Therefore, I urge you, brothers and sisters, in view of God's mercy, to offer your bodies as a living sacrifice, holy and pleasing to God—this is your true and proper worship. Do not conform to the pattern of this world, but be transformed by the renewing of your mind. Then you will be able to test and approve what God's will is—his good, pleasing and perfect will."

These verses highlight four steps for the reader in discovering God's "good, pleasing and perfect will." To begin, the phrase "in view of God's mercy" opens the passage by drawing attention to our focus. Everything we do should be through the lens of what Jesus did for us on the cross. This should be the heart of our concentration and motivations.

So **step 1 is simply to focus on the cross.** As we pray over a dream, selfish ambition fades away at the sight of the mercy shown at Calvary. Focusing on the cross shapes our perspective. Our dream no longer becomes only about us. It no longer prioritizes materialistic, admired, or self-seeking gains. Instead, it views its goal as an investment into eternity. No matter the dream, the question should be asked: Is this about me or him?

Step 2 in discovering his will is to die to ourselves. Romans says that true and proper worship is to offer our bodies "as a living sacrifice, holy and pleasing to God." The natural outcome of focusing on the cross is to offer ourselves completely to him in full, unrestrained worship. Worship then isn't only a song we sing; it is the lifestyle we live! In worship, we surrender ourselves and all earthly, momentary gain for his pleasure and his eternal purpose. In worship we continually echo the question of twentieth-century evangelist Leonard Ravenhill: "Are the things you are living for worth Christ dying for?"

The road to significance is paved with sacrifice. When we offer ourselves to God, we give him our desires for both laziness and legacy. We give him our tendencies to drift and to be driven. Both ends of the spectrum belong to him. When we offer ourselves to God in true and proper worship, we realize this isn't really about us at all. In Romans 6:22, Paul used the term "slaves of God" to describe all of us who have been set free from sin. In worship, we gratefully choose this title, as the verse goes on to say that "the benefit you reap leads to holiness, and the result is eternal life."

Moving to step 3, after focusing on the cross and dying to self, we now change our pursuit. Paul said, "Do not conform to the pattern of this world, but be transformed by the renewing of your mind." A pursuit after the world will look very different from the pursuit after God. This is where Joseph's brothers misunderstood his dream. They believed Joseph was pursuing dominance. But in God's kingdom our aim is never selfish; it is always service. We dream of a platform not so that we can shine but so that we can serve.

What is your motive? So that you can adequately assess this question in your own heart, let me ask again. What is your motive . . . really? Why do you want that platform . . . really? What do you hope to get from success . . . really? David prayed, "Search me, O God, and know my heart! Try me and know my thoughts!" (Ps. 139:23 ESV). If your goal is to gather followers, you have the wrong motives. If your goal is a larger bank account, you have the wrong motives. If your goal is fame or recognition, you have the wrong motives. We will never be able to trust our movement until our motives are right. Take a moment and search your heart as you prayerfully consider what is driving you.

We fix our motives by renewing our mind. When our mind is drawn to a negative pattern or desire of this world, we take immediate action. Second Corinthians 10:5 charges us to "take captive every thought to make it obedient to Christ." If the thought is not in God's mind, I refuse to let it in my mind. As our minds are renewed by the Holy Spirit, we are transformed. We are now operating with the mind of

Christ (1 Cor. 2:16), gloriously able to discern a path with his wisdom and his guidance.

To review, here are the steps in seeking to discover God's will:

- **Step 1**: Focus on the cross
- **Step 2**: Die to ourselves
- **Step 3**: Change our pursuit

Now, in step 4, we can walk with confidence. Paul said, "You will be able to test and approve what God's will is." As our focus, our worship, and our motives become centered on him, we can be confident that we are now operating with his wisdom and understanding. So, as we pray, we can discern with assurance if this dream is for now or later, or maybe even not at all.

In my own life, I have experienced this confidence that only comes from the Holy Spirit. I am so thankful for it, because when my big dreams needed God-sized miracles, I stood with confidence that I knew his will. I walked with faith that God had said it, and if God had said it, then I was going to believe it.

Practically, one clear signal I look for when I am in a season of prayer over God's will is a continued urgency that does not let up. In other words, if you can't shake it, start it. We have this idea that everyone has these same audacious plans of stepping out in faith and achieving the impossible. They don't. Joseph was the minority. His brothers definitely were not comparing God-inspired goals with him. Instead, he was ridiculed and ostracized and left frustrated by his dreams. Let this encourage you. If you feel like you don't fit in, it's because you aren't supposed to.

Here is some good news. Nowhere in Romans 12:1–2 are you told to poll popular opinion on whether the dream given to you is possible. You don't need other people to believe in you for God to believe in you. Joseph's brothers didn't choose him, but God did. I think it is important that we celebrate each other, but I am not counting on that. If God spoke to you, if you can't shake the idea, if you know you are made for more, then stop trying to fit in.

TOO OLD TO DREAM?

Joseph's great-grandfather, Abram, had been given the dream of a son. His dream became God-sized when God promised him—at age ninety-nine—that a son would finally come soon. Ninety-nine years old! God changed Abram's name in that moment to Abraham, meaning "father of a multitude." So, after waiting so long, not only would he and his elderly wife finally have a child together, but he would be known as the father of many. God spoke and said, "I will make you very fruitful; I will make nations of you, and kings will come from you" (Gen. 17:6). Abram could have looked at his pattern. He could have let his years of disappointment or his physical age convince him that this promise was out of his reach. Instead, he dreamed of his God-given potential. Within a year's time, Abraham's ninety-year-old wife gave birth to their son, Isaac, who eventually fathered Jacob, Joseph's dad. Jacob's twelve sons became the twelve tribes of Israel and God's chosen people throughout the Old Testament (Deut. 7:6). Additionally, Galatians 3:29 says, "Now that you belong to Christ, you are the true children of Abraham" (NLT). So Abraham's legacy grew from barrenness to a son, to a highly favored nation, to the family of all who believe in Christ. He definitely became the "father of a multitude"! We can all learn from Abraham. Dreaming big is not just about us, it is about the legacy we will leave.

Abraham's story challenges us to never stop dreaming. Moses was eighty when he began his life mission of delivering the children of Israel by confronting Pharaoh to let God's people go. If you think that's old, Noah was at least five hundred when he took on the challenge to obey God by building a giant boat. Far too often we think our best days are behind us, and we end up drifting into eternity instead of dreaming about legacy.

It is not too late for you to dream big. Ray Kroc, the famous developer of the global McDonald's conglomerate, didn't purchase his first restaurant until 1961, after he passed his fifty-ninth birthday. Sam Walton, founder of Walmart, opened his first store when he was forty-four years old. Nelson Mandela became the president of South Africa at age seventy-six. Harland Sanders, the founder of Kentucky Fried Chicken, was sixty-two when he franchised KFC.[2] Thank God none of them quit. Purpose does not stop because of age. You are never too old to dream big.

Whether you are 10 or 110, God wants to dream through you. Acts 2:17 gives the encouragement, "'In the last days, God says, I will pour out my Spirit on all people. . . .

Your young men will see visions, your old men will dream dreams.'" By the power of the Spirit, younger people can be veered by vision and older people can be driven by dreams. It is this same Spirit that revealed to Joseph the potential God had for him.

In a world that pursues safe goals, I want to encourage you to pursue God-sized dreams. These dreams are windows into what is possible if we submit ourselves to his plan. Pastor Robert H. Schuller is said to have wisely remarked, "You can often measure a person by the size of his dream." I would take it a step further and say, "You can often measure a person's destiny by the size of their dreams."

Joseph may have been young in age, but he was big in dreams. Being a ridiculed dreamer, especially at a young age, is unfair. Joseph wasn't satisfied with only doing what other seventeen-year-olds were doing. He dreamed of significance exceeding the norm. He dreamed of influence. He dreamed of standing out. Sound familiar? I am sure at some point in your life you realized you have been called to something great. You know you are here for more than the mundane. You have been created *on* purpose and *for* a purpose.

MAKING THE DREAM A REALITY

The road of a dreamer may consist of many unfair stops; however, every movement forward is inspiring. The advantage becomes noticeable when a dream is given action. You have good intentions behind your dreams, but without action they are only fantasy. I've often heard there is no straight line to a dream.

The Lord spoke through the prophet Habakkuk to "write the vision; make it plain on tablets, so he may run who reads it" (Hab. 2:2 ESV). A dream has the potential to move from fantasy to probable as soon as you "write the vision." It doesn't become real until it's written. This practice has worked for other big dreamers. Shipping magnate Aristotle Onassis once said, "Always carry a notebook. Write everything down. . . . That is a million-dollar lesson they don't teach you in business school!"[3] Billionaire investor Warren Buffett described writing as the key to making ideas a reality.[4] Even well-known entrepreneur Richard Branson has been known to travel with a school notebook, which he throws ideas into.[5]

Writing down a dream has multiple benefits. When someone important is talking, people show honor by listening intently and taking notes. The same is true when a dream is written. We honor God, the Dream Giver, by showing him the value we have placed on what he has said. Notetakers are world changers.

Writing down a dream is also an act of faith. James 2:26 reveals the harsh truth that "faith without deeds is dead." Hearing God is useless if we never take his next step. Until you do something about your dreams, they are good for nothing. So, as an act of faith, start writing down the things you are believing God for. For years I carried a dream in my heart of one day writing a book. However, it remained only a figment of my imagination until the day I put it into words. I penciled the idea into my calendar and set a date to begin making it a reality. I had to move some things around to make it work, and I questioned how I would accomplish something that seemed so huge. But if I always treated the dream as impossible or inconvenient, what would I really be saying to the Lord?

Another benefit of writing is that it deepens our understanding. The more you write, the more you understand. This is why, almost every day, I journal during my devotional times. I use the SOAP method of Bible study (Scripture, Observation, Application, Prayer). You can google this method if you are interested. While reading my Bible, I find a scripture to focus on, and then I follow with "writing it down." As I spend time writing through the SOAP process, the passage becomes clearer. I continually gain new insight and deeper understanding of God and his Word through this practice. Similarly, writing down a dream can enhance the vision of it and can often help reveal the next steps that should be pursued.

Writing it out also helps me remember it. The shortest pencil always beats the longest memory. About ten years ago, I wrote down a page of bucket list goals I would like to achieve in my lifetime. In the past decade I have been able to check many of them off; however, many other items remain that I hope one day to accomplish. If I had not written these down, I don't believe I would have done many of them or known what I was aiming for next. Routinely examining this list gives me renewed focus on where I am directing my life.

Many dreamers thrive on the intensity of new dreams. They are fresh and full of the excitement of what's to come. There is something to be said, though, about plowing the field of an old dream with consistent faithfulness. Consistency does not receive a lot of accolades when talking about good virtues, and yet it is a character attribute that makes us more like Christ. He "is the same yesterday and today and forever" (Heb. 13:8). God's purpose does not change based on his feelings, and neither should it change based on ours. So writing goals down keeps the focus on his assignment long after the feelings of excitement leave.

I've learned the key is to dream big but start small. As that beautiful vision of your dream is laid before you, realize there will be a process to get to it. Unfortunately, many people do not accomplish the big things because they are unwilling to do the small things necessary to get them there. As nice as it would be, there is no easy elevator to your goal. You usually have to take the stairs. Dreams become reality one faithful step at a time.

In the beginning of 2012, life was good. My wife and I had just bought our first home and were expecting our first child. We had two incomes, a few vacations planned, and a great group of friends nearby. But then the big dream happened. I was happily serving at our local church in Pensacola, but I couldn't shake this idea of starting a new church in the city of Tampa. It was such a bizarre dream that it had to be from God.

Katie and I started taking steps to pursue it. We prayed, and researched, and read, and had conversations, and went to trainings, and put action into the dream. For one whole year we took little steps that eventually led to our making a massive move. With a six-month-old baby, an overly hyper dog, and a U-Haul, we uprooted our entire lives and moved in faith to Tampa.

Following the move, another season of small steps awaited us: talking to church planters, sitting in trainings, learning the ins and outs of branding and marketing, coming up with a name, creating a website, establishing our mission and values, building a team, raising money, finding a facility, developing the culture, and the list goes on and on. The larger-than-life dream was composed of thousands of small steps. Everything from the outside looked exciting, but the behind-the-scenes work was exhausting.

Many people dream, but few are willing to go through the steps to make their dreams a reality. I wonder how many people have missed the opportunity to experience the fullness of their God-sized dream because they became discouraged on the path to get there. Archaeologist and author T. E. Lawrence said, "All men dream: but not equally. Those who dream by night in the dusty recesses of their minds wake up in the day to find it was vanity, but the dreamers of the day are dangerous men, for they may act their dreams with open eyes, to make it possible."[6] Keep your eyes open and your mind sharp. Be intentional in your dreaming, constantly on the lookout for opportunities that will make that goal a reality. If you don't invest wisely in your dream, you will spend your life working for someone else's.

Today I am sitting at a hotel on a beach overlooking the Gulf of Mexico. I have been working intently the past few days turning an outline into a book. It's not lost on me that this season in my life is not ideal for this. In the midst of a global pandemic, our church has been in a constant state of trying to navigate everything to be as healthy as possible. It has been challenging and time-consuming, and launching a new location has added to the activity. On top of this, my wife and I had a new baby a few months ago. Needless to say, our house is a little chaotic at the moment. So why am I here? Because the dream will never become a reality unless I take intentional steps to make it happen. You don't find time—you make time.

There will always be an obstacle. There will always be a reason why the dream seems impossible. This is the unfairness. Don't fall for it though. Your advantage is right around the corner. What small step can you take today to work toward your dream?

BEING ALL THERE

One of the most challenging frustrations for those who dream is continuing to remain present while holding on to vision for the future. Dreamers tend to have their minds on what is next instead of on what is now. But as we dream, we must be careful not to focus so much on *there* we end up not being effective *here*. A quote by missionary Jim Elliot has been one of my life mantras and has helped me stay grounded when my mind wants to run a million miles ahead. "Wherever you are, be all there."[7] A tension exists between the hope of future possibilities and the desire to live fully present, but effective world changers have learned to manage this tension well. It is possible to be a future thinker while also being present-focused.

There is a power in being present. Unfortunately, most of us are everywhere, except for where we really need to be. We are overextended, overcommitted, and overconfident in our belief that we can handle it all. It is said that time is measured in minutes, but life is measured in moments. Busyness keeps us from experiencing those moments that we truly need the most. That special memory with our kids, that important life lesson, the vacation that would have empowered us for the next season are all easily dismissed for the sake of busy tasks. I catch myself often missing out on great things because I am distracted by good things.

I have five children. Each one is uniquely different and special. As they continue to get a little bigger every day, my dreams for them get bigger too. I dream of how they will grow up to love Jesus and how each of them will use their own unique callings to change the world. These dreams are good things, but my problem is focusing so much on their future that I am missing out on their present. Even as I am writing this book, my four-year-old son keeps walking into the room and begging for my attention. It is a constant balance of being intentional in the present while also investing in the future.

THE UNFAIR ADVANTAGE: KEEP DREAMING

In Genesis 37, we learn the already simmering hatred in his brothers intensified when Joseph told them about his dream. Verse 8 says, "They hated him all the more because of his dream and what he had said." When confronted with animosity, it becomes all too easy to allow other people's opinions to dictate the direction of our dreams. We may give up, shut down, or believe we misunderstood our assignment. This is a mistake. People should never determine our potential; only our Creator has the right to do that.

In response to his brothers' hurtful reactions, Joseph could have chosen to stop dreaming. He was misunderstood and misjudged by his family and could have decided to live according to their expectations and ideals. This isn't what he did though. Immediately after we see his brothers' hatred in verse 8, Genesis 37:9 tells us how Joseph responded: "Then he had another dream." Joseph kept dreaming. This is his unfair advantage.

Dreams are the foundation on which greatness is built. When you stop dreaming, you start dying. Irish playwright George Bernard Shaw knew this concept when he said, "I want to be thoroughly used up when I die."[8] We don't live for earthly retirement. We live for eternal rewards. If you are still living, God is still dreaming through you. If you have a pulse, God still has a plan.

What negative thoughts or words have you let pour water on the fire of your dreams? Far too many people navigate by the opinions of others rather than by the guidance of God. Sadly, those who live for the opinions of men will die underneath their criticisms. You can please God, or you can please man. Seldom can you do both. Joseph made the powerful choice to keep his eyes on God and the dream in his heart.

In the late 1700s, a young minister named William Carey felt a deep burden for those in other countries who did not know Christ. Full of passion over this need, he bravely shared his heart with other ministers concerning the need for overseas missionaries. Surely, these men of God would feel a similar passion. But instead of championing his dream, they criticized. One seasoned pastor called him a "miserable enthusiast" and told him that God would reach people in his own way without the help of any man, including William.

Refusing to let the rebuke quench his passion, Carey became even more determined to follow his call. He understood that resistance was to be expected, so he continued to work hard, sharing his dream and pushing through setbacks, until he eventually formed a society for missionaries and was able to move to India as one himself.

As a result of his perseverance, William Carey's legacy still lives on today. He worked to translate the Bible into almost forty languages, founded a university that still exists today, and saw a substantial impact in the gospel being spread throughout the Indian subcontinent. Carey's most famous quote exemplifies his remarkable life: "Expect great things from God; attempt great things for God."[9] I am so glad that William Carey kept dreaming despite the opinions of those around him.

Dreams are bigger than man-made ideas. Therefore man has a hard time comprehending them. So when a dream is criticized, keep dreaming. When a dream looks like it is over, keep dreaming. When you are getting older, keep dreaming.

Do not merely take a cautious step toward a dream fragment; instead, wholeheartedly pursue your big dreams.

Sometimes people disassemble their dream into a fraction of what it could be. One reason is because of the concern of what people will think. The target is lowered so we are not embarrassed if we miss it

> When a dream looks like it is over, keep dreaming.

on the first try. We play it safe so no one will see us fail.

Also, our own flaws and frailties can seem so large and intimidating. We stop taking steps forward because moving past our weaknesses seems impossible. As believers, however, we are free to cast all of these things aside as our focus shifts from ourselves and onto God's power at work within us.

The apostle Paul had many dreams as well as many deficits. For this reason, he must have been so encouraged when the Lord said to him, "My grace is sufficient for you, for my power is made perfect in weakness" (2 Cor. 12:9). This is good news for all of us. His power is not limited by our shortcomings. Learning to lean on God is always the first step in going from the natural to the supernatural. And so, turning toward him and trusting in him, we are able to chase after the dream that is so much bigger than we are. H. Jackson Brown Jr. challenged us by quoting what his mother told him: "Twenty years from now you will be more disappointed by the things you didn't do than by the ones you did. So throw off the bowlines. Sail away from the safe harbor. Catch the trade winds in your sails. Explore. Dream. Discover."[10]

If the dream fails, if the critics are loud, if you are misunderstood, here is your unfair advantage: keep dreaming.

Joseph had a second dream. Maybe *you* need some time to get a second dream, not to let the opinions of others dictate the direction of your life. What is God speaking? I can bet on the fact that his best is still ahead of you. If you have a pulse, he still has a plan. Dream again.

DISCUSSION QUESTIONS

We all have obstacles to our dreams or reasons why we should not dream again. Take some time and answer the following questions to apply the lessons learned in this section. With the right application, dreaming again can be used for your advantage.

1. What are the dreams that you can't shake?
2. What do you feel are the obstacles to fulfilling your dream?
3. What criticism has kept you from believing the dream is possible?
4. What is the motive behind your dream?
5. What are some steps you can take today to start the process of making your dream a reality?
6. What would be your legacy if your dream was fulfilled?

THE REDIRECTED REJECT

So it came to pass, when Joseph had come to his brothers, that they stripped Joseph of his tunic, the tunic of many colors that was on him. Then they took him and cast him into a pit. And the pit was empty; there was no water in it.

GENESIS 37:23-24 NKJV

A few years back, I was given the opportunity to preach at a youth conference in New Zealand. The country is beautiful. I spent a day riding mopeds through the mountainside, avoiding all the sheep in the road. The most recent statistic is that there are seven sheep to every one human in New Zealand.[1] But it wasn't the sheep that shocked me. It was the birds.

None of the birds in New Zealand fly. They look like

birds, have wings like birds, but they don't fly like other birds. I did some research and found that birds in New Zealand are flightless because they have no predators. No snakes, no spiders, and no large animals that would attack. (What a paradise. If I sell enough of these books, I might just go ahead and retire in Auckland.)

Because nothing is chasing them, the birds are not motivated to leave the ground. In their comfort, they have forgotten how to fly. So what seems like paradise has become a prison. They can't experience what they are created to experience. Only the existence of predators pushes a bird to get off the ground and into the sky.

In the same way, opposition becomes your friend when you let it push you to greater heights. Your dream is not going to come to pass without opposition. So how do we deal with the opposition coming from those closest to us? Haters on social media don't hurt us nearly as much as a lack of support from the people we love and trust. In this chapter we will deal with an unfair part of life every world changer encounters: rejection. You take hold of your unfair advantage when you learn how to deal with rejection. You can get sour, or you can get soaring. Be frustrated or start flying. Stay low or stand tall. Cower back or let it push you to the next level. The choice is yours.

REJECTION HAPPENS

Joseph's life became even more unfair when he experienced the pain of deep rejection from his family. His dream caused such an intense anger in his brothers that they plotted to hurt him to the point of death. Seventeen years of family memories and brotherhood could not save Joseph from their hatred. Those who should have been there to help him tried to kill him. Instead of unconditional acceptance, Joseph received ultimate rejection.

More than his dream was rejected. There was also the much more personal rejection of Joseph as a human being. It is hard enough when our ideas, skills, words, or plans are turned down. It is a completely different level of hurt when we are rejected based on who we are as an individual. Joseph was slammed face-first with this hurtful realization. But before his brothers had a chance to rid him from the world completely, they had a moment of clarity and decided to throw him into a pit instead. *How kind of them.* Interestingly, the pit that is mentioned in Genesis 37:24 is described as being empty. What a fitting word for a season when the people who are closest to you decide to cancel you. The pit of rejection is the emptiest of places.

No one has completely escaped the pain of rejection. Everyone has a story. *It's unfair that he cheated. It's unfair you were fired. It's unfair that the kids don't want a relationship. It's unfair that your parent walked out. It's unfair you were dumped so close to the wedding. It's unfair that the company never called back. It's unfair that those you tried so hard to please hurt you in return.* It is very unfair, but it is also very expected. Rejection is a normal part of life.

It sometimes feels like no one has suffered the pain of rejection like we have. However, here is a list of well-known people who would tell us differently.

Walt Disney was rejected from multiple newspaper companies because he "lacked imagination and had no good ideas."[2]

Oprah Winfrey was rejected from her first job as a reporter because they believed she was too emotional. The producers wanted her to separate her emotions from the stories she was telling.[3]

Thomas Edison was fired after his secret, late-night experiments resulted in a fire that damaged his company's property.[4] He took this as a sign to start inventing. Most of Edison's inventions did not work, but he was persistent.

Joe Biden was rejected twice as a US presidential candidate before winning the presidency on his third try in 2020.[5]

Michael Jordan was rejected from his high school basketball team. Later, after going professional, he said, "I have missed more than 9,000 shots in my career. I've lost almost 300 games. 26 times I've been trusted to take the game-winning shot and missed. I've failed over, and over, and over again in my life. And that is why I succeed."[6]

Rejection happens to the best of us, but it doesn't have to get the best of us. You can live unoffendable in an offensive world. Can we be honest? People can be mean. There is no hurt quite like people hurt. And we have all felt it.

In the first year of our church plant, we had a board member come to the hospital after my second daughter was born. For the past year we had been doing life with this man and his wife. We had gone out to eat many times, attended birthday parties together, prayed together, and dreamed together. So, on this very special day, I believed that he had shown up to celebrate our new baby girl. As soon as he walked into the room, however, he immediately pulled me aside and told me we needed to talk. While his wife admired our brand-new baby, he decided this was the moment to begin verbally attacking me as a person. I sat there for forty-five minutes as he gave example after example of how terrible I was. He ended by saying I was a bad leader and he would be leaving the church. In case you didn't catch it, let me remind you that this was during the first few hours of my daughter's life. I learned a lot in that moment. First, I needed to set some personal boundaries; second, rejection hurts.

REJECTION HURTS

Who else suffered through the sting of rejection as a middle schooler? Allow me to tell you a little about my experience. When I was going into sixth grade, my family decided to move from Baton Rouge, Louisiana, to Pensacola, Florida. Not only was this a new city, a new state, and a new home for me, but I was also the new kid at the local Christian middle school. That is a *whole lot* of transition during one of the most awkward ages in a person's life. It was crucial that I find a way to fit in and make friends fast, so I decided to try out for the sixth-grade basketball team. There were so many kids in our grade that an extra team was created, so it was pretty much a guarantee I would make the cut.

Unfortunately, tryouts didn't go as well as I had hoped. I was tall for my age, but I was also extremely awkward. My lankiness didn't help when it came to actually dribbling the ball or making baskets. Nevertheless, after two days of tryouts, I was sure I was going to make it. I vividly remember walking up to the coach's office and seeing that piece of paper posted on the window listing the roster. There were so many names to scroll through as I looked and looked, the whole time thinking the next name must be mine. Sadly, after going through the list again and again, I finally realized I hadn't made the team. The crushing feeling of rejection at a time when I needed to find acceptance the most hit me deeply. To add insult to injury, I soon discovered I was one of only two people who didn't make the team. Two! I was so hurt.

My sad basketball saga doesn't end here. The next year for seventh grade I moved to an even smaller Christian school and was determined to have a fresh start. This meant giving basketball another try. "If at first you don't succeed . . ." (or so I was told). This school was so small that they were begging the guys in my class to try out. The coach even got really excited about my height and made me promise I would show up. You probably can guess by now that the tryouts were equally as bad as the year before. The roster was posted. This time only nine guys tried out. Eight made the team. I could not believe that I was the one not chosen. The only one! In my mind, the least they could have done was let me on the team so I wouldn't be so humiliated. The coach sent me a clear message that day that I wasn't even good enough to sit on the bench. I was devastated. Rejection hurts.

Research done on rejection reveals it to be more than just getting your feelings hurt. MRI studies show that in the event of rejection, the same areas of the brain become activated as when we experience physical pain.[7] This could be because we are created to belong, and the inability to find acceptance within a community will ignite genuine pain. From the beginning God said, "It is not good for the man to be alone" (Gen. 2:18). The first crisis in Scripture wasn't sin; it was solitude. The Enemy uses rejection as a tool to get us isolated and alone.

Those who know you best are often those who can hurt you the most. Rejection from a troll on social media is far less hurtful than rejection from a family member or friend. The closer the relationship, the deeper the cut. How do people usually respond to these wounds? We fight back. For example, my wife is the most loving and kind person on the planet. Years ago, before I realized that she is a little claustrophobic, I trapped her under a blanket as a joke. What surprised me most was when my sweet-natured wife turned into a wild woman, kicking and punching around to save herself. Many times, the same kind of reaction can be seen when people are mentally wounded by others. They hit and kick to try to save themselves, often hurting others and themselves in the process.

The US surgeon general released a report that noted "rejection was a greater risk for adolescent violence than drugs, poverty, or gang membership."[8] Wow! It is true that hurt people hurt people. The internal pain of seeing parents divorce, watching a loved one leave, suffering a breakup, losing a job, overhearing slander, or many other acts of rejection can take such a toll on our health and our actions.

Rejection can be hard to make sense of because in our minds we would never treat someone the hurtful way we are being treated. For example, if I were that basketball coach, I would have just put me on the team. Leaving only one guy out is harsh, but that is the problem with humanity. Too often people see things through their own perspective and not through the lens of those around them. Joseph's brothers genuinely thought getting rid of Joseph was the best decision, because they were thinking only of themselves.

Selfishness is a cancer to all relationships. It kills marriages, ruins partnerships, and destroys friendships. Selfishness makes us stop looking at people as a treasure from God and instead as a tool for our use. Selfishness convinces us that people are no longer our companions—they are our competition. We treat others the way we would never want to be treated.

I have been on both ends of rejection. I have given it and gotten it and know from experience that being on the receiving end is much more damaging. If we could just remember the pain we felt when we were betrayed, we would be so much more cautious not to inflict that pain on others. This world would be a much kinder place if we lived by Jesus' golden rule, "Do to others what you would have them do to you" (Matt. 7:12). A simple question to ask yourself is "Would I want someone to do this to me?" That question can go a long way toward how we view and appreciate others.

REJECTION IS EXPECTED

A man in our community has been a huge part of helping build our church since the beginning. The two of us have traveled the globe and ministered together. He is the kind of guy who will show up in an instant to lend a hand, and everyone loves him.

In the summer of 2019, this friend received devastating news about his marriage that shocked everybody. How could something this terrible happen to someone with such innate loyalty? Many times, the kindest people get the unkindest treatment. That is a harsh reality of our fallen world. No one is perfect and there are always two sides to every relationship that goes south or to every broken marriage. But there are definitely cases where one person in the relationship bore the brunt of unfair, unjust treatment. I've seen marriages end when one person in the relationship consistently did their level best to be faithful and honest and make things work, only to be met with reckless indifference, unfaithfulness, and abandonment from the other person. One person's selfishness leads to the devastation of a family.

Think of this situation with Joseph. He was given a coat by his dad and he shared some of his dreams about success. In response, his brothers became insanely jealous to the point of murder. The verdict didn't fit the crime. Joseph found himself on the bad side of man's selfishness when his brothers cast him into an empty pit. You might say that is an extreme example. I would say it is an expected outcome.

Jesus told his followers, "Brother will betray brother to death, and a father his child; children will rebel against their parents and have them put to death. You will be hated by everyone because of me" (Matt. 10:21–22). This verse usually isn't one I underline or put on my fridge as a reminder.

It does not feel good, but it is factual. Jesus went on to say, "If the world hates you, keep in mind that it hated me first" (John 15:18).

If anyone deserved to be accepted, it was Jesus. How can you not love Jesus? He ministered to the hurting. He healed the sick. He taught a message of love and compassion and truth. He offered unending hope. Yet the very crowds that celebrated him one week crucified him the next. Be careful how much stock you put in the praise and celebration of people. If you are upset that not everyone likes you, take heart; you are in good company.

The rejection of Jesus didn't come only from a crowd of outsiders. In three years of ministry, Jesus ministered to thousands, but he mentored merely twelve. Each of these men should have savored the closeness of Christ, vowing to cling to him no matter the cost. However, on the hardest night of his life, Jesus was rejected and completely betrayed by Judas, one of the Twelve. Out of fear for their lives, his other close friends abandoned and denied him, running away from him in his final hours. The night Jesus needed his friends the most, one of them was working behind his back to have him killed while the others put their own needs ahead of his.

When Jesus was dying on the cross, the Roman soldiers took a spear and pierced his side. The Bible tells us blood and water flowed from his side. Multiple books and articles have been written on the idea that Jesus died not because of the effects of crucifixion, but based on a heart attack, something that was triggered in the garden. Doctors have referenced the passage in Luke where Jesus was in such distress that "His sweat became like drops of blood, falling down upon the ground" (Luke 22:44 NASB). C. Truman Davis wrote, "Though very rare, the phenomenon of Hematidrosis, or bloody sweat, is well documented. Under great emotional stress, tiny capillaries in the sweat glands can break, thus mixing blood with sweat."[9]

It is believed that Jesus' heart began to fail in the garden, not because of the torture of the Roman crucifixion but because of the betrayal of those who loved him the most. What could have caused such an overwhelming stress response? Could it be he was thinking of something other than the physical torture he knew would soon take place? Take a look at Jesus' cry from the cross recorded in Matthew 27:46: "About three in the afternoon Jesus cried out in a loud voice, '*Eli, Eli, lema sabachthani?*' (which means 'My God, my God, why have you forsaken me?')." In order to take our sins upon himself, there was this moment on the cross when God the Father had to turn away from Jesus, separating him from the Father's presence. I believe this time of abandonment from the one he had been in perfect relationship with for eternity was that moment Jesus had been dreading. This is what caused the hematidrosis in the garden, and this possibly even could have led to his heart failure. Although the rejection was necessary in this ultimate act of love, it was still excruciatingly painful.

Rejection can be expected in the life of faith. Moses was called by God to free the people from their slavery in Egypt. What did Pharaoh do? Rejected him. Then when Moses cast vision to the Israelite people, what did they do? Acts 7:35 says they rejected him with the words "Who made you ruler and judge?" Ouch! David was anointed as king over Israel. What was King Saul's response? Rejection and attempted murder. Samson fell in love with Delilah. What did she do? She told his secret to his Philistine enemies, betraying their relationship, and ultimately leading to his death. The Bible is filled with stories like this.

When I recommitted my life to the Lord at the age of sixteen, I knew my future would be in full-time ministry. With my call to ministry also came this strong desire to preach God's Word for the rest of my life. My Christian high school had a chapel that, once a year, was led by students. I believed this could be my first preaching opportunity. So when my teacher asked our class who would like to speak that year, my hand quickly shot up. I was called to do this! I just knew I had a message people needed to hear. Although he tried to be nice about it, my confidence was crushed when my teacher told me I would be better at giving a short devotional between the worship songs.

I knew that was just an afterthought position for someone who could not be taken seriously. The knife sunk deeper when the person who was chosen had no desire to preach at all. I put my all into that devotional, but inside I harbored the hurt that no one believed in me or thought I had what it took for the task I had been created for. It was so unfair. I wondered how no one could see the potential in me. It could have been very tempting to believe that maybe I was mistaken about my calling. Maybe everyone else could see what I couldn't, and I really wasn't qualified or capable.

Since then, I have gone on to preach over five hundred different sermons in the last fifteen years of ministry. It is humbling to think that some of those messages have been used in church small groups and shared in front of auditoriums with thousands in attendance. It could have been so easy to let that high school rejection paralyze me, but instead, I let it propel me toward God's ultimate plan for my life. I was knocked down, but I got back up. That rejection in eleventh grade prepared me for a life of not always winning.

DIRECTED BY BEING REJECTED

Rejection is full of pain, but it can also be full of purpose. Joseph was sitting in an empty pit, probably entertaining a lot of resentful thoughts against his brothers, when a caravan of merchants came through. Scripture tells us, "When the Midianite merchants came by, his brothers pulled Joseph up out of the cistern and sold him for twenty shekels of silver to the Ishmaelites, who took him to Egypt" (Gen. 37:28). Twenty shekels of silver was equal to about a month's worth of work. A strong, healthy seventeen-year-old boy would have been worth so much more than only a month of income. So they not only sold him, but they sold him for cheap. Talk about hurt.

Joseph would travel an astounding 250 miles before reaching his new life in Egypt. The road of rejection is long and lonely. Every bump across that rugged territory must have been a reminder of the betrayal of his eleven brothers.

Before an age of cell phones and email, Joseph had to have thought there would be no chance he would ever return to his home in Canaan.

What Joseph didn't know was that man's rejection would end up being God's direction. God didn't cause Joseph's rejection, but he did use it. He navigated that hurtful sale for something bigger than Joseph could see in that moment. Joseph's pain was necessary to bring about his ultimate purpose.

It reminds me of baby birds that get pushed out of their nest. It's a painful but necessary process for them to eventually fly. In a similar way, God used Joseph's corrupt brothers to push him toward his incredible assignment. Maybe he has been using your pain to nudge you toward your ultimate calling as well.

Often when God gives a promise, the path to it looks nothing like what you thought it would. Think of Moses. God promised him a beautiful land filled with milk and honey. The path to it, however, was filled with struggle, rejection, and forty years in the wilderness. In your own life, don't be discouraged if the path isn't as easy as you had hoped. Those rough places could be the preparation ground you need for the promise ahead.

Things do not have to make sense for it to be God. I will repeat that to make sure you get it. *It doesn't have to make sense for it to be God.* Actually, a lot of times, if it is God, it won't make much sense at first. Joseph had a dream that he would be royalty. Who would have thought his brothers' treachery would be the catalyst to get him there?

THIS IS NOT WHAT I EXPECTED

My wife and I moved to Tampa to start a church in 2013. We had so many dreams of what our church should look like. So we searched high and low for a state-of-the-art facility with a spacious room, lots of impressive lights, room for an LED wall, comfortable seating, and a massive stage.

The local high school was the perfect setup. It had the look, the space, the parking, and the amenities that checked off all our boxes. Most importantly, it was at ground zero of the community we were trying to reach. For six months we believed for this school. We did prayer walks around it in faith (while also being really careful not to look like awkward creepers walking around a school). For the past decade the school had refused to have a church in their facility, but we were still hopeful and faith-filled. Even as we continued to hear "no" in conversations with school administration, we still believed God would open a door. This was the building we had dreamed of; this was what we had in mind when we uprooted our lives and moved to a strange city; this was what we believed God had been calling us to. We got within six weeks of our church launch when we received the final word: a definite, unchanging no. It was such a disappointing rejection.

So at the last minute we found a run-down, dirty dollar movie theater a mile up the road. The owner said we could launch the church in their two-hundred-seat auditorium. It smelled like a mixture of mildew and popcorn. You could literally hear rats running across the drop ceiling. It was definitely not our dream and was far from the first impression we wanted guests to have on our opening Sunday. My hopes were dashed. I felt like I had inherited a second-class version of the call God had for me in Tampa. Joseph probably felt a similar way in the back of that caravan. The dream he saw was not the reality of his experience.

The opening day for our church was not what I pictured. We had a great turnout, but the sound was terrible (a used sound system purchased from Craigslist is never a good idea), we ran out of seats, the sermon was not my greatest, and everything smelled like dirty popcorn. Things didn't get any better after the launch.

One week while I was preaching, there was a commotion in the back of the room. I thought the crowd must be overwhelmed with excitement for the sermon. I had heard stories of famous revivals where people couldn't even stay in their pews because of conviction. Unfortunately, that was not the scenario for us at Radiant Church. Come to find out, during the closing of my message a rat fell from the ceiling and was running across the floor.

Despite all of these glitches, I tried to stay positive. But every week for the first few months of our church, the number of people in attendance kept decreasing. I felt like every time I preached, fewer people came. This was definitely not our dream.

It was a hard start in a place we did not want to be. However, a few years after we began renting the theater, we were given an incredible opportunity that we never would have had otherwise. In the community we are in, real estate is extremely hard to get. Finding a location to rent was very difficult. Finding a location that would be permanent was next to impossible. That is why we see God so clearly in what happened next.

A few years after renting that dirty dollar-theater auditorium, we were able to miraculously take over the lease to the entire theater, giving us an unexpected permanent location. This was twenty-five thousand square feet of prime real estate in the heart of the community we were trying to reach. Once we obtained this, we were able to fully renovate the space into everything we had been dreaming, and the church exploded in growth. Now, every weekend that one location facilitates thousands of worshippers. Looking back, it is easy to see how every no was God's nudge to his greater plan. Man's rejection leads to God's direction.

> **Man's rejection leads to God's direction.**

CHAIN OF EVENTS

This story is one of the reasons I wrote the book. It is my personal Joseph story. One of the most memorable rejections in my life happened at the end of my eleventh-grade year of high school. I have to be honest: I wasn't the kind of student who teachers love to have in class. Disrespect and the desire for attention meant I was constantly in trouble with my teachers and the school administration. I became a regular in after-school detention. It was a normal part of my routine.

I had begun pulling away from my faith when I entered

high school. Then, during tenth grade, I became friends with some guys who led me even further from the Lord. With these guys I got drunk for the first time and soon became familiar with the party scene. My buddy's dad was a medical doctor, and with the buffet of pills he provided, I started using prescription drugs to get high. I have since lived by the maxim "Show me your friends and I will show you your future." These guys were setting me up for a tragic ending.

That summer after my sophomore year, I went overseas on a mission trip. My mom, who is my hero, encouraged me every summer to go somewhere. I love to travel, and missions were my excuse to see the world. So that summer of 2000 I ended up in Nepal for one month. God transformed my life on that trip. I recommitted my life to him and was called into ministry. That moment has marked my life for the last two decades. I consider it the greatest turning point in my life. God changed my life and I suddenly had an urgency for him to use me to change the world.

God's plan doesn't always work according to our timeline or expectations. It can take a lot longer than we want it to. Going from a crazy teenager who was in detention every week to a church planter, seeing thousands of lives impacted for eternity, was a slow process filled with a lot of rejection along the way.

Those guys I partied with were the first to reject me. They quickly ditched me after making sure they first told me I was taking this Jesus stuff a little too seriously. This was a really lonely season, so to find some good friends, I started to spend more time in my youth group. It was there that I was encouraged to start a Bible study on my high school campus.

I had never been in any type of ministry leadership, and honestly, I wasn't sure what I was doing, but to my amazement the study was a huge success. It was probably that people were so shocked at the extreme difference between who I had become compared to who I was a year before that they stuck around just to see if my passion for God would stick. Thankfully, it was there to stay, and as my hunger for God continued to grow, my Bible study grew as well.

Sadly, my school principal continued to see me only as a troublemaker. Nothing, not even this high school ministry, could change his mind. I knew he didn't like me, so I wasn't surprised when he suddenly called me into his office one day. He used the Bible study against me, saying if I was going to lead, then he was going to have to hold me to a higher standard.

There was no grace or compassion in his voice when he told me that if I received three more detentions, he would expel me. It was obvious what outcome he wanted. Sure enough, the next few months were nothing short of a witch hunt. One man's personal vendetta against a teenage boy ended with my receiving three more detentions and then finally getting expelled during my last month of eleventh grade.

After being escorted like a criminal off the campus, I never returned again as a student. My heart hurt that day. I had just made some really awesome new friends, I had been elected senior class president for the coming year, and I was starting to excel in ministry. How could one man's rejection ruin so much? I hated every day of my new school. With only one more month left in the school year, no one was interested in making a new friend. There were many days I ate by myself in the bathroom just so no one saw me eating alone. Talk about humbling.

My old Christian school had been my mission field, but when that was ripped away, I began to ask God what I should focus on now. I learned all about dual enrollment through our local junior college. This had not been an option for me before, but now at this public school I went to work, using my senior year of high school to start knocking out college courses. Little did I know how this would pay off. I was able to finish college in three years instead of four, and on the day of my graduation, the missions professor told me about a newly listed opportunity to serve in disaster relief efforts in the country of Sri Lanka. I would be working with five thousand orphan children, helping them learn about Jesus. It was a dream opportunity, available only because I had graduated a year earlier than I should have.

I learned so much in Sri Lanka and continued to experience the call of God in my life. After a year overseas, I launched a thrift store in Pensacola to help raise necessary funds for churches throughout Asia. While overseeing the thrift store, I was offered a job as a youth pastor at Brownsville, the church I had spent so much time in as a teenager.

Although I had not seen myself in this type of ministry, it turned out to be an incredible blessing. The time spent, the people met, and the highs and lows of being a youth pastor were all imperative steps to where God would end up using me later as a lead pastor. And six years after I was escorted off that high school campus as an expelled student, I walked back on as a youth pastor who was asked to preach in one of their chapel services. It's crazy how God is able to turn things around for good.

Let's review together the chain of events. I would have never been where I am as a lead pastor if I had not first been offered the job of youth pastor. I would have never been offered that job if I hadn't opened a thrift store in town. I would have never opened the thrift store if I hadn't gone to Sri Lanka. I would have never gone to Sri Lanka if I hadn't graduated from college a year early. I would have never graduated early if I hadn't done dual enrollment. I would have never done dual enrollment if I hadn't gotten kicked out of my high school. I would have never been kicked out if one man hadn't decided to dislike me. Boom! Man's rejection moved me in God's direction. Can you see any rejection chain of events in your own life that God has worked for good?

BITTER OR BETTER?

How is your heart? This could be the most important question you answer today. The heart is actually referenced 633 times in the Old Testament and 170 times in the New Testament. God has a lot to say about its condition. The health of your heart determines the health of your life. So to get an accurate measurement of how healthy you are, take a deeper look at two areas. The first question to ask yourself is "How am I acting?" Proverbs 27:19 tells us, "As water reflects the face, so one's life reflects the heart."

The second question to ask yourself is "How am I speaking?" Jesus teaches in Matthew 12:34, "Out of the abundance of the heart the mouth speaks" (NKJV). Do you find your words laced with complaining, negativity, or criticism? This may indicate a problem with your heart.

Undergoing rejection will have a significant impact on your heart's condition. You have a choice in the matter though. Use the rejection to get *bitter* or use it to get *better*. Rejection can be the poison that sinks us to bitterness, or it can be the fuel that drives us to greatness. We all know people who have used their rejection experience poorly. Left in the frozen state of perpetual hurt, bitterness oozes out of them, creating discomfort and hurt for the people around them. Choose wisely how you want rejection to affect you.

Rejection happens to the best of us, but it doesn't need to get the best of us. So how do we fight that innate bitterness that tries its hardest to creep in? Scripture tells us: "Above all else, guard your heart, for everything you do flows from it" (Prov. 4:23). What you allow into your heart when you are rejected will determine its condition.

Unforgiveness is a toxin to the heart. Refusing to forgive is choosing to stay trapped in a jail cell of bitterness, serving time for someone else's crime. I am not sure who originally said that, but it is very true. (And I'm not worried about stealing that quote because that person has to forgive me!)

In the midst of extreme suffering, while he was still at the peak of his torment on the cross, Jesus made the crucial decision to forgive. He didn't wait until their murderous act was over but faced his betrayers and critics and, while they were inflicting pain, imparted forgiveness. He forgave before the offense had a chance to infect his heart. Despite his agony, he mustered his last bit of energy and cried out, "Father, forgive them, for they do not know what they are doing" (Luke 23:34).

Jesus has given us the perfect example to follow. Ephesians 4:32 instructs us to "be kind and compassionate to one another, forgiving each other, just as in Christ God forgave you." We don't deserve it, but Jesus forgave us. Now we have no choice but to forgive others in return.

Offense can be a festering wound to our hearts. No matter how we try to escape it, our world can be very offensive. People say things that hurt. People do things that hurt. People overpromise and underdeliver. People cut you off in traffic, renege on money they owe you, and disappoint your expectations. Hurtful things happen on a daily basis. However, it is possible that offensive things can happen *to* you without the offense living *in* you.

An offense is an event. Becoming offended is a choice. Joseph had a decision to make in the back of that caravan. In the famous words of Elsa from *Frozen*, Joseph had to "let it go." Holding on to hurt is exhausting and detrimental to your heart. If you have noticed unhealthy patterns occurring as a result of rejection, let me encourage you to take the steps necessary to release the offense so you can move on.

The number one killer in America for the past decade has been heart disease. I believe the number one killer of your potential is spiritual heart disease. Don't become a casualty.

Be intentional to guard your heart as well as purify your heart from the hurt caused by life. You can go through bitter situations without becoming a bitter person. In a moment of rejection, rather than taking it personally, choose to see people as Jesus did, who forgave the highest offense with the words "they do not know what they are doing" (Luke 23:24).

LET GOD HEAL YOUR BROKENNESS

There is an old Japanese legend dating back five hundred years of a man who was a leader in the Japanese military, otherwise known as a shogun. Legend says that one day he broke his favorite teacup. Unwilling to accept it as lost, he determined to repair it to even better than before. He picked up every shard of the broken cup and painstakingly pieced it back together. For the final touch, he sealed the cracks with gold, making the cup more precious than it had been before. In other words, instead of getting bitter, he got better.

Whether or not the story is true, the art form is alive today in the Japanese practice of *kintsugi*. Take a moment to google some images. Just like in the legend, the kintsugi artist breaks an intact pottery object, allowing it to shatter into dozens of pieces. The artist then begins the work of placing all of the broken pieces back together. When the pieces are replaced, instead of glue or tape, they are sealed with gold. In doing this, the kintsugi artist gives broken pottery way more value than it had when it was still undamaged.

Here we see a powerful lesson of redemption. In the hands of the artist, the artifact goes from broken to beautiful. In short, "the Japanese art of kintsugi teaches that broken objects are not something to hide but to display with pride."[10] This is the gospel. Jesus owns our brokenness and gives it intrinsic value.

Is your heart broken? Rejection can often do that. The only lasting solution is to give your pieces to the Master Artist. The prophet declared, "We are the clay, you are the potter; we are all the work of your hand" (Isa. 64:8). When we place our brokenness in his hand, he lovingly turns it into something beautiful. Our brokenness moves us from a mess to a message. Our hurt transforms into healing for other people. Our frustration changes into fuel for the future. None of this is possible in our own hands.

God is the only one who can change our hearts. He promises, "I will give you a new heart and put a new spirit in you; I will remove from you your heart of stone and give you a heart of flesh" (Ezek. 36:26). Before you read on, allow him to do some heart surgery and heal some of those broken places, so, like Joseph, you can move into "Egypt" better instead of bitter.

THE UNFAIR ADVANTAGE: LOOKING AT REJECTION AS REDIRECTION

The rejection from Joseph's brothers must have wounded him greatly. But little did he know how significant it would be. Rejection, when handled properly, can become one of your greatest resources. It can move you toward the ultimate purpose God has for your life. It was necessary to move Joseph to Egypt.

Rejection can become one of your greatest resources.

So how do we use rejection for our advantage? Rather than allowing it to be a hurdle keeping us in our past, we turn rejection into the fuel that propels us to what is next. Two people can go through the same rotten situation, but while one emerges victorious, the other leaves completely defeated. The difference in these two people is *attitude*. How you decide to handle your hurdle will either fuel you for good or frustrate you to despair. It is your choice.

Here are four great questions to ask yourself amid rejection. These questions will help you navigate from something being unfair to being an unfair advantage. When you ask yourself these questions, put the word "really" at the end of them. This will help you evaluate if you are being honest with yourself.

- **Question 1: Am I holding on to bitterness?** My first step toward being redirected amid rejection is to release bitterness. It doesn't let your abuser off the hook, but it frees you to walk into your destiny.
- **Question 2: What could I have done differently?** Every great leader is a great learner. Your best lessons will be from your haters. When someone leaves my church or quits my staff, the first thing I do is look inward to see how I could have handled it better.

- **Question 3: Do I need to try again?** As you saw in chapter 1, many times the victory comes after trying again and again. It takes faith to move on, but it also takes faith to try again when all looks lost. Great leaders know when to keep fighting, and they also know when the horse is dead and it is time to dismount.
- **Question 4: What is the next opportunity?** If God is pushing me out of the nest or away from my comfort zone, then there is an opportunity on the other side I haven't seen yet. It is time to get creative.

One of the major lies people tend to believe is that adversity will keep us from our destiny. Nothing could be further from the truth. What seems like a loss is always for our gain, if we just give it enough time. It seems extreme, but I truly believe we need to receive rejection in order to reach our ultimate potential.

Joseph found himself in a pit. While he was sitting alone in the darkness, he may not have considered his rejection helpful. Just like that empty pit, rejection is an empty season. The good news, however, is that, as in Joseph's life, the pit is not the end of your story. It's just a part of it. Rejection might have thrown you into a dark, empty pit. But take a breath and consider this just a pit stop on your journey. Grab a Slurpee and some peanuts. Remind yourself that this is temporary and that God will move you on to greater things.

When we get to the end of Joseph's story, he confronts the very people who rejected him. It had been over a decade since he'd seen his brothers, and he was now in a position of power over the very people who had tried to ruin his life. He easily could have taken revenge. If he spent those years letting his wounds fester, it would have been very tempting to attack and get even. Instead, he saw his rejection as the path that brought him to his potential. He looked at the very brothers who had so cruelly rejected him and said, "You intended to harm me, but God intended it for good to accomplish what is now being done, the saving of many lives" (Gen. 50:20).

It might be thirteen days, thirteen months, or thirteen years later, but like Joseph, you *will* look back and see how man's rejection moved you toward God's direction. Yes, the road is painful, but it is also full of so much purpose.

There is nothing fair about rejection. I don't want to minimize its anguish. I know well how hurtful it is. That is why there is so much hope in knowing how God uses all the pain for our advantage. It's for our good! So if you have been rejected, be encouraged. It could be that God is moving you toward something spectacular.

It's unfair, but it's for your advantage.

DISCUSSION QUESTIONS

Rejection can be extremely hurtful. Take some time to reflect on your experience(s) of rejection. Make sure you give Jesus the pieces to your broken heart, and trust that he will put them back together with such care and precision that your value will only increase.

1. What rejection has most defined your life?
2. Who is the person who has rejected you the most?
3. Have you released your bitterness to the Lord?
4. What do you need to do to move past the hurt?
5. How has God used rejection to become a chain of events to lead you toward his ultimate direction?

UNFAIR ADVANTAGE #3

THE WAGELESS WORKER

*Now Joseph had been taken down to Egypt.
Potiphar, an Egyptian who was one of
Pharaoh's officials, the captain of the guard,
bought him from the Ishmaelites who had
taken him there.*

GENESIS 39:1

One of the great lies we teach ourselves is rooted in an entitle-ment mentality that success is hard for us but easy for everyone else. This distorted perspective is amplified by social media. I bought into this lie for years. We judge our behind-the-scenes fights against everyone else's beautifully filtered highlight reels.

I always thought I was given a bad hand when it came to different areas of my life, especially school. My friends could goof off in class, avoid studying, and still get straight As. I had to work hard, study a bunch, and I was barely a C student. I hope this encourages all the C students out there. I have finished my master's, completed my doctorate—including a 187-page dissertation—and now I am writing a book. You can be a C student and change the world. (That should be your quote of the day).

When I decided to start a church, I went to a training in Birmingham. I had no clue what to do. This room was filled with the coolest-looking pastors I have ever met. Katie and I were not prepared for this event. All the other churches had slick websites and fundraising materials ready. We didn't even know the name of our church or what city we were moving to. Everyone always seemed to be a step or two ahead of us. Story of my life. These couples made starting a church look so easy. I thought it was hard for me, but easy for them.

This is a lie. People might make it look easy, but truly accomplishing greatness is extremely difficult for everyone. With a few exceptions, we have all been given a sound mind, a healthy body, and the same twenty-four hours in a day. No one is going to hand you greatness. You have to work for it. The more I got to know these fellow church leaders in Birmingham, the more I was inspired by their hard work. None of them had it easy. None of them were being handed a ministry. They all understood their church was going to happen only with the combination of God's grace and their hard work.

I have always heard it said, "Work smart, not hard." That is not possible. The world belongs to those who will work both the smartest and the hardest. All business start-ups are funded by some sweat equity of the founder. Jeff Bezos had a vision of launching the world's largest online bookstore. Where did it start? His garage. The equipment for Amazon pulled so much power from his house that his family couldn't run a hair dryer or vacuum because it would trip a fuse.[1]

Bezos expected his employees at the start of Amazon to follow his model and work a minimum of sixty hours a week. The employees worked smart, but they also worked hard. When people see Amazon today, it looks like they have it easy. Anything that looks easy in public is built on intense labor in private.

In my opinion, Michael Jordan is the GOAT of the basketball world. No offense to all of my LeBron or Kobe fans. Jordan made it look easy. We discussed earlier how he did not make his high school basketball team, but what I didn't say is how hard he worked to make himself the most well-known and highest-paid athlete on the globe.

A *Business Insider* article summarized Jordan's work ethic: "It was hard work that made him a legend. When Jordan first entered the league, his jump shot wasn't good enough. He spent his off-season taking hundreds of jumpers a day until it was perfect."[2] Good genes do not make you the best in the business; hard work does.

Let me just throw out some other inspiring info I found in the same *Business Insider* article:

- Starbucks CEO Howard Schultz often works thirteen-hour days and then works more once he returns home.
- Mark Cuban, who owns the Dallas Mavericks, went seven years without a vacation when he was launching his first business.
- Jeffrey Immelt, the CEO of General Electric, worked one hundred hours per week for twenty-four years.
- Tim Cook, Apple's CEO, regularly is up and emailing other employees by 4:30 a.m.
- Chinese business billionaire Li Ka-shing left school at age fifteen and started working in a plastics factory. He worked himself up to general manager at nineteen and eventually started his own company, worth over $21 billion today.[3]

Stop expecting someone to hand you success. Your life might have started bad, but it doesn't have to end bad. It might seem unfair that you didn't have a trust fund handed down to you, parents to mentor you, shoulders to stand on, or a spouse to help you. I get it. But the fact is, with a bit of hard work, you can accomplish the dreams God has put in your heart.

Roll up your sleeves. Put in a little sweat equity. I might not be the smartest in the group, but others are not going to outwork me. One of my favorite quotes on hard work is sometimes credited to football legend Vince Lombardi: "The dictionary is the only place that success comes before work. Work is the key to success, and hard work can help you accomplish anything." I hope you are challenged to work harder than ever before.

SOLD INTO SLAVERY

After Joseph's brothers betrayed and sold him, Genesis 39 transitions to Joseph's new life in Egypt where he was sold to a man named Potiphar. Verse 1 mentions specifically that Joseph was bought from the Ishmaelites, reinforcing the truth of his new identity as a purchased slave. Slavery of fellow human beings is one of the darkest and most depraved parts of our history. This is the scenario Joseph found himself in.

Imagine with me the anguish Joseph must have experienced in that two-hundred-plus-mile journey to Egypt. After a life of comfort, being doted on as a favorite child, he was now chained and put into the back of a caravan—or possibly forced to walk every grueling day it would take to reach their destination. The slaves imprisoned beside him may not have spoken his language, making communication impossible. His feelings of isolation increased at the lack of connection with another human. The unknown of his future and the risk of death in his present may have created constant anxiety, making even those few moments of permitted rest difficult. Food and water were limited to survival rations, possibly resulting in the beginning effects of starvation and dehydration.

He arrived in Egypt starving, weak, and suffering physically and mentally from the journey. He heard the hustle and bustle of the Egyptian market, knowing that he was now as much of an object for sale as the items being haggled over around him. As he saw the pyramids off in the distance, the truth solidified that this was his new life and everything he once knew was gone.

Joseph was dragged, along with the other trafficked individuals, to a small platform. The bidding began. Fear struck his heart as he realized this moment would determine his fate. Who would buy him? What kind of work would he end up doing? How could his brothers do this to him? Maybe a slight ember of hope remained as he looked out on the crowd, wanting to see his father or his brothers, wishing they had followed the caravan and were there to rescue him. Instead, the faces before him were indifferent, greedy, and hateful.

On that day, a captain in the Egyptian army named Potiphar happened to be looking for some extra help around his house. He had recently been promoted and had the extra funds to hire (buy) the staff needed to take care of his multiple affairs. He was looking for a strong young man who could handle responsibility. In this market Potiphar spotted Joseph. He made the final bid, and Joseph now belonged to him.

In what must have felt like a nightmare, Joseph went from the favorite of his father's twelve sons to a common slave in an Egyptian home hundreds of miles away. He had zero freedom, zero authority, and zero influence. However, through the darkness we see a glimpse of light in Genesis 39:2: "The LORD was with Joseph so that he prospered."

Even in Joseph's most difficult moments, God never left

him. Equally true, God has never left you. The psalmist wrote, "The LORD is close to the brokenhearted and saves those who are crushed in spirit" (Ps. 34:18). You might feel alone, but you are not alone. Some of the most impactful moments I have had with God were when I embraced a season of loneliness and turned it into alone time with God. When others are far away, that is when God leans in close. My friend and youth pastor legend Jeanne Mayo taught me, "Loneliness is for your benefit when it forces you to draw companionship from God that you would normally try to draw from other people."

During heartbreak, loneliness, suffering, and the unfamiliar, God is there. When it feels like everything is out of control, God is there. When the future seems bleak or blurry, God is there, and he can always be trusted. During World War II, a remarkable Christian woman, along with her family, courageously hid many refugees from the Nazis in their home in the Netherlands. After being discovered they were arrested and imprisoned. Although several of her family members died, the woman, Corrie ten Boom, survived the brutality of the concentration camp she was sent to. Her experience only strengthened her faith in God, and upon being freed she traveled the world, sharing her story along with the gospel. Corrie had grieved, she had suffered, and she had been in the darkest circumstances imaginable. And coming out of it, she wisely said, "If you go on a train journey, you first find out which train you need to take. If you are on the right train, you don't need to worry about red and green lights; the engineer takes care of that. . . . The Lord Jesus is the engineer. Place your trust in Him."[4]

The best thing you can do during uncertainty is to trust your unknown future to a known God. He promises to walk with us even during the darkest times. David wrote, "Even though I walk through the darkest valley, I will fear no evil, for you are with me" (Ps. 23:4). Is this a dark time in your life? Can I encourage you? God is near you. God is with you. You can prosper in the midst of a painful season. Even if the situation is over your head, you are still in God's hands.

CHOOSE YOUR ATTITUDE

Galatians 5:13 says, "You, my brothers and sisters, were called to be free." There is a craving inside human beings for freedom. As a slave, however, all of Joseph's independence was stripped away. No longer could he go where he wanted or say what he wanted. No longer could he eat, dress, or live the way he wished. If I were Joseph, I would have been angry. I would have walked around all day pouting, always thinking about what could have been. Joseph had no freedom, but the one choice that continued to belong to him was his attitude.

You cannot choose your adversities, but you can choose your attitude. It is a choice that you must intentionally and continually make.

> You cannot choose your adversities, but you can choose your attitude.

As your attitude goes, so goes your life, your relationships, your parenting, your job, and so on. In aviation, the word *attitude* is actually used by airline pilots to describe a plane's horizontal relationship with the runway. If the plane's attitude is correct, then it is aligned properly and can soar to 30,000 feet. If the attitude is wrong, it will lead to a crash.

In the same way, your attitude affects your altitude. Even in negative conditions, when your attitude is good, you can soar higher than ever before. You can shift the atmosphere simply by shifting your attitude.

Joseph's season in slavery began with the right attitude. Christians should always have the best attitudes. Paul challenges us to "have the same attitude that Christ Jesus had" (Phil. 2:5 NLT). I have to remind myself of this often. The world is watching. Our attitudes might be our greatest argument to prove that God is with us. Boom!

I cannot have a positive life with a negative attitude. I also believe you cannot have a negative life with a positive attitude. Attitude is everything. Joseph chose an attitude that propelled him to an eventual promotion.

WORK ETHIC

"When his master saw that the LORD was with him and that the LORD gave him success in everything he did, Joseph found favor in his eyes and became his attendant. Potiphar put him in charge of his household, and he entrusted to his care everything he owned" (Gen. 39:3–4).

Joseph stepped into this role at Potiphar's house with a work ethic that would set him above everyone else. This may have been developed at an early age as he was taking care of sheep for his father. Wherever it came from, it is fair to say Joseph was a hard worker.

Working hard for pay is normal. Working hard as a slave is unfair. But little did Joseph know that hard work, no matter the situation, would bring him closer to God's perfect plan. I hope over the next few pages to encourage those of you who work hard but see little results. You might not feel it right now, but your hard work will eventually pay off.

Growing up in the Burke family did not guarantee my brother, sisters, and I would have the sharpest mind or the highest IQ. But we all inherited a crazy-hard work ethic. Both of my parents modeled the apostle Paul's challenge: "Whatever you do, work at it with all your heart, as working for the Lord" (Col. 3:23).

It did not matter if it was selling cars or picking weeds, Burke kids learned to get things done no matter how hard it was. Despite how successful my parents were, we never expected things to be given to us. We knew that "if you want it, you have to work for it." In order to save enough money to buy a car, I got my first job at McDonald's when I was fifteen years old. My dad owned a car business, but there was no way he was giving me a car for free. He could afford it, but it would not have been a wise investment in my future. One of the greatest values you can teach your child is to work hard. Show up early, stay late, and bring your best.

Far too many people have million-dollar dreams and a hundred-dollar work ethic. They may have the right heart, but they lack the hustle. Success is not easy. Young people are often done a disservice when presented with the idea that it is. Anything that is easy has already been done. If you want to do something great, do what is difficult and work hard.

DO WHAT OTHERS WON'T DO

I once heard John Maxwell speak on work ethic and say, "We have uphill hopes and downhill habits."[5] I couldn't have said it better. What you consistently do determines what you eventually become. Our destiny is defined by our daily decisions. It's not a matter of dreaming; it's a matter of doing. The difference between those who do something and those who don't do something is that those who do something, do something. Profound, isn't it? Get to work.

Someone once said, "We often miss opportunity because it is dressed in overalls and looks like work." This was the situation Joseph was handed. He was purchased as a slave but took it as an opportunity to shine. The result? He was put in charge of Potiphar's home. Productivity precedes promotion. If you work at it long enough and hard enough, someone will eventually notice and you will get elevated.

Joseph did not to do the bare minimum. He did what others wouldn't do, and so he got the promotion others didn't get. He could have embraced the victim role. In fact, he was a victim of human trafficking. In that light, Joseph should have put his attention toward lying low, going unnoticed, and eventually escaping. But he took another approach.

Joseph made the most of the opportunity given. As a

result, he found favor in his master's eyes. Potiphar bought Joseph as a slave but ended up making him his personal attendant. This was a high honor. Why was Joseph promoted? Simple: he did what others didn't do.

I hear often, "When I get my dream job, then I will put in the effort." "When I get married, then I will settle down." "When I get kids, then I will start a budget." "When I become a business owner, then I will show up early or stay late." That is not how it works.

If you wait to work hard until you have your dream job, you will never get your dream job. Hard work doesn't follow perfect opportunities—it creates them. You don't work hard when the right door opens; you work hard, and the outcome is that the right door opens.

Joseph discovered the power of hard work and I hope you do also. When you grind and hustle in a job you hate, you position yourself for the job you want. This is the secret to success. And if it looks easy for other people, it is probably because they put in twice the amount of hard work behind the scenes that you can't see.

When we planted the church, I knew I had some major unfair obstacles. I had never done this before and was new to the entire church planting world. I knew the only thing that would set me apart was doing more than the average planter. I couldn't outsmart people, but I could outwork them.

I would interview pastors who had gone before me and started churches across America, and I would ask them their plan. If they told me they invited ten people a week, I would try to invite fifteen. If they sent out a 60,000-piece direct mailer, I would try a 75,000-piece. If they raised $50,000, I would aim for $80,000. I knew if I wanted results that were different, I needed to do something that was different.

Churches had started in the South Tampa community before, but none survived in the decade before we launched. The only option I had was to remove any bit of entitlement and apply some serious hustle. No one owed me success. No one was going to hand it to me. If I wanted to see results other people didn't see, I would have to do things no one else was willing to do.

Hard work has now become a staple of our staff and leadership culture. I would challenge you to make it a part of your life. Christians are not saved because we work hard, but we are saved to work hard. Because our mission is so crucial, we are willing to put in more time and energy than other people. If we do what others are unwilling to do, maybe we will get the results they were unable to achieve.

TAKING INITIATIVE

A foundational trait of hard workers is that they take initiative when others simply do not. I am a firm believer that initiative can be taught. It was modeled by my parents and my youth pastor growing up. You can learn the art of taking initiative and it can set you apart, like Joseph was, in your industry. Initiative is the difference between the average and the achievers. You are called to be an achiever.

Initiative is the ability to recognize and do what needs

to be done before being asked to do it. It is human nature to take the path of least resistance, the fastest shortcut. Because everyone is doing the minimum, taking initiative is your best way to shine in your organization. When you take initiative you take ownership of your progress by becoming proactive in getting things done.

Taking initiative means going the extra mile and completing a task without a directive given by your boss. As someone who manages dozens of employees, there is no greater quality I look for in those I am trying to promote. Taking initiative means taking responsibility for your own success.

Here is a simple way to apply this to your current situation: if you see a need, meet the need. God does not reveal problems for us to complain about them, but for us to change them. I am not an agent of complaints. I am an agent of change. Some of you need to repeat that statement every morning.

As a pastor, I find that people regularly approach me with ministry ideas. I love their heart to see more people reached or to see the church continually improve. People are filled with great ideas. I always give the same response when they present the problem, stating my belief in them that *they* can start that ministry or serve in that area. My job, according to Paul, is to "equip the saints for the work of ministry" (Eph. 4:12 ESV). If you present me a problem, I am going to suggest that you are the solution. "If anyone, then, knows the good they ought to do and doesn't do it, it is sin for them" (James 4:17). A lack of solving the need you see is actually categorized as sin. This raises the importance of taking initiative to another level.

A couple of ladies in my church came to my office a

few months back and told me about a huge crisis in the current foster care system. They not only came to me with problems, but they came with potential solutions. They laid out a detailed plan of how they could lead an initiative within our church to mobilize hundreds of young families to solve this crisis. I was so blown away by their initiative. We, of course, took on the project, and lives have been transformed because of it.

Here are four areas where I challenge people to take initiative.

First, take initiative with your boss. If you are a student, you could replace the word "boss" with "mentor" or "teacher." This relationship needs to be a priority. Do not wait for them to come to you; pursue them. Pursue them for one-on-one meetings. Come prepared with great questions. Present goals to them for your department and make sure you are staying aligned with his or her ultimate vision. One of the easiest wins with your boss or mentor is to take initiative by getting to know them and their family. My favorite people care about my favorite people. Learn their kids' names and what hobbies make them come alive.

Second, take initiative with departmental improvements. Everything should improve wherever you are involved. If there is a problem in your department, fix it. If the problem is in your department for an extended period of time, the problem is not the problem, the problem is you. I know that hurts but it is true. Many times the longer we are in an environment,

Learn to solve problems no one else can solve.

the fewer issues we see. Time *in* erodes awareness *of*. Focus a fresh set of eyes on what you are doing and see how you can take initiative to make your area better. Problem solvers are promotable. Learn to solve problems no one else can solve.

Third, take initiative with organization-wide improvements. Move from an employee mindset to an ownership mindset. The way I treat a hotel room is different from the way I treat my own room. The hotel room is left dirty, I throw towels on the ground, and I wouldn't even think of repairing something that is broken. Why? Because I don't own it. I am a temporary visitor. When it is my house, every room is my responsibility and I treat each part with care. This is how you should handle the company you are part of. When the organization wins, you all win. Operate as an owner. Give healthy feedback across departments and watch how your initiative will start to be noticed.

Fourth and finally, take initiative with your personal growth. Many times the hardest person we are called to lead is ourselves. I hope this book is a catalyst for growth, but in the end, I am not responsible for your growth—you are. When is the last time you took initiative for your growth? I challenge myself often to set stretching yet measurable goals. I do them in three major time frames: daily to-do lists, yearly stretch goals, and lifelong bucket list goals. I know other people break their yearly goals down into quarters. Whatever works for you. Just don't defend what isn't working.

It takes faith to write down a goal. To better focus my goals, I write them into five categories: spiritual, physical, relational, influential, and experiential. No one tells me to write these down. I take initiative. No one told me to write a book. I got the dream from God, wrote it on my life goals bucket list, and set out some time to write it. What are you waiting for? Take some initiative with your life and get some goals. Make sure they stretch you. They need to be faith-filled. But they also need to be measurable. Your initiative shouldn't be "I want to lose weight." You have to make that goal measurable: "I want to lose five pounds."

Let me be vulnerable with you: at times I lack the energy and passion to take initiative—especially after a season of defeat when I am feeling discouraged. One of my favorite passages in Scripture is when David and his army reached the town of Ziklag to find it burned down and two of his wives captured by the enemy. David's army turned on him and was ready to kill him. The Bible tells us, "David was greatly distressed because the men were talking of stoning him; each one was bitter in spirit because of his sons and daughters. But David found strength in the LORD his God" (1 Sam. 30:6).

David discovered the key I have held on to throughout the last two decades. He found his strength in the Lord. When you feel defeated, discouraged, or demotivated, take a five-minute, five-hour, or five-day retreat and get alone with the Lord. He will encourage you and strengthen you to take the initiative you need. Remember, if God placed you in a mess, maybe he knows you have the ability, with his grace, to manage it. I do not succumb to dysfunction, I solve it. I take initiative.

NO ONE SEES ME

If there were ever a time to slack off, it was after Joseph was sold into slavery and eventually purchased by Potiphar. Forget making minimum wage; Joseph wasn't making a dime, or you could say he wasn't making a shekel. Not only was he not making any money, but no one was watching over his shoulder. His father didn't see him, his brothers weren't observing him, and possibly Potiphar wasn't around most of the time. There was no money and no management. Time to take your foot off the gas. But that is not the approach Joseph took.

Joseph was put in an unfair situation with unfair compensation, but he worked at it like it was his dream job. Maybe this is why we have struggled so much in our careers. We make hard work about what others see instead of what God sees.

What if God is waiting to see how you react to the job in front of you before he gives you the job destined for you? What if God is watching your diligence in the small and few to see if you are able to handle the management of the many?

Jesus challenged his followers in the famous Sermon on the Mount to practice what we now call spiritual disciplines. In a matter of a few verses, he challenged his followers to pray, fast, and give. All three are difficult and all three are to be done in secret. Why? "Then your Father, who sees what is done in secret, will reward you" (Matt. 6:4). When you do the right thing, God will promote you. It is the same with your workplace. When you do what is right, you can expect promotion.

I have worked different jobs, but I have never worked my jobs differently. Read that sentence again; I think it is actually pretty profound. I walked into every job with the expectation that this was my favorite job and the place I will spend the rest of my life. I walked into McDonald's as a teen with the clear expectation that I would be the owner of a bunch of McDonald's. I was working as if my future depended on it. Your future is not the sum of your intentions; it is the sum of your actions.

You should approach every job, every task, every season with the foundational declaration that "I am going to work at it with everything I have." I don't work hard because the task is valuable; I work hard because I am valuable. It is unfair to be underpaid, or even not paid at all, for our hard work. But pay cannot be your motivation. Don't pursue pay. Pursue a pattern of hard work. Pay will eventually follow hard work.

Let's be real: we have all been in seasons where we have worked jobs that are different from our ultimate dream. This is unfair, but this is life. I served as a youth pastor for six years before starting our church seven hours away in Tampa. Youth ministry was not my goal, nor was it really my passion. But it was the assignment God put in front of me.

If you want what is next, you have to start with what is now. The hidden years of youth ministry prepared me for the very public years of ministry I have experienced. God prepares us in private and eventually displays us in public.

If your dream is not in a mature state, it is probably because you aren't either. Let him continue the work in and through you, even if no one sees it. What you do with the small determines what God can trust you with when he hands you the large. I would suggest to you that maybe God is watching to see how you handle what has been directed before he releases what is desired.

I have caught myself saying, "I will start to work hard when I get to the dream I originally saw." This is a trap. What I originally saw at sixteen years old on that side of the hill in Nepal was huge. I saw me preaching the gospel to thousands of people, seeing lives transformed around the globe. The years that followed, even the decades that followed, have been only a fraction of the potential I saw in that original dream.

My internship at the end of college was in a suburb of Portland, Oregon. It was in a small Assemblies of God church that had a great pastor who invested heavily into my life. He asked me what I felt called to do, and I told him I wanted to be a preacher. A month or so into the internship, he gave me my first opportunity to speak on a Sunday morning. Their church had just been given oversight of a small congregation in St. Helens, Washington. He told me they didn't have a worship team, so I would need to take a couple of the youth-band members and put on the Sunday service. I was ready. I must have put thirty-plus hours into the study portion of that message. I wanted these people in St. Helens to get the best of Aaron Burke.

It took about ninety minutes to travel from Beaverton, Oregon, to St. Helens. I was so nervous. I don't think I have ever prayed that hard before a message. I brought four people with me: two to help with worship, one to be my "armor bearer," and one came for moral support. This was an old-school church position. It basically was a groupie that would follow me around, hold my Bible, and get me water. It was a pointless role.

We arrived at the small white church in the middle of town a few hours early. I went to the back room and paced back and forth while the worship team warmed up. I decided to go out a few minutes early. I didn't want to be the preacher who walks out after worship has already started. Five minutes before the service, and not a single person had shown up. I walked out to the parking lot to make sure there was no parking issue. Nope. No issue at all, mostly because there were no cars parking.

When the clock struck 10 a.m., the time for the service to start, we had no one in the audience. I told the worship team that we would just wait because I was sure people would show up. And sure enough, they did. Cars started pouring in. Let me clarify. Two cars pulled in. Between the two cars, there were seven people. By the time I got up to preach, there were eleven people in the audience. I had brought four of them.

I am probably the only person who remembered the message from that Sunday. I didn't care if anyone else was in that audience. I wasn't preaching for them. I was preaching for God. He was my audience. The year before the COVID-19 pandemic, our church rented out the Tampa Convention Center and packed it out with thousands of people in multiple services. I can promise you I preached just as hard to those eleven in St. Helens as I did to the thousands in downtown Tampa.

It is a fun story to share now that I am seventeen years down the road. I drove off from that church super discouraged. Why didn't more people show? My senior pastor wasn't even there to hear my message. I never got a chance to preach the rest of the summer. I was bummed. In seasons where we feel like no one sees us, we have to trust the words of Jesus: "Well done, good and faithful servant! You have been faithful with a few things; I will put you in charge of many things" (Matt. 25:23). Many things come after faithfulness with few things.

The fruit I am reaping now is from seed I sowed years ago. Want to get depressed? Plant a seed and sit there and watch it grow. It will drive you crazy. Here is a better idea: plant a seed and trust it will grow in the right time. My next opportunity to preach a Sunday morning service was in a village in the middle of Sri Lanka. There were around thirty adults in attendance, three times the amount of St. Helens. I was faithful with a few, and God brought the increase.

Private faithfulness brings about public fruit. Everyone wants the spotlight. Few want stacking chairs. Both are ministry. Currently God has given us a vision called 10k for Tampa Bay. We want to launch ten campuses reaching ten thousand people a weekend by our ten-year anniversary. It is an audacious goal. I believe it will happen. I am just not waiting to bring my best until it does happen. I am leading, preaching, praying, and growing now with the same effort that I will when our church is double the size.

If the season handed to you is not your dream, look at it like an investment. Every month, money is deducted from my bank account and put into a 403(b) retirement account. It frustrates me not to have that money, but I trust my investor that I will be able to pull it out one day and use it to enjoy some of the finer things in life. It is the same with your current platform. Trust your Creator. Give your best right now. It is an investment in your future. It might not be fair that you are underpaid or undervalued. But God will be faithful to his Word. "Do not be deceived: God cannot be mocked. A man reaps what he sows" (Gal. 6:7). If you sow laziness, you will reap lack. If you sow hard work, you will reap a harvest. You invest, you will inherit. It is the law of sowing and reaping. It works 100 percent of the time.

MY WORK IS MY WORSHIP

Hard work is not just practical, it is also very spiritual. Hard work not only prepares you for greatness but it also positions you to give God glory. Paul wrote, "So whether you eat or drink or whatever you do, do it all for the glory of God" (1 Cor. 10:31). God is glorified when we bring our best to whatever situation we are in. I am not working for man. I am working for God. He deserves my best. No one knew this more than Joseph.

Joseph had no one to impress other than his God. When no one was looking, he was working for an audience of one. Your hard work doesn't feel like hard work when you are doing it for the God of the universe. Because I belong to him, everything I do is worship. How I treat my wife, worship. How I prepare for a message, worship. How I react when I get cut off in traffic, worship. How I approach my day-to-day job, worship.

Worship is given to many things. We worship whatever has our time, attention, and money. The great tragedy in the church is that we have made worship synonymous with singing. Worship isn't synonymous with singing; worship is synonymous with sacrifice. Worship should never be taken casually or lightly. We can have a "casual" worship environment without making worship cheap.

I am afraid that because we have made worship about singing, we have downgraded the value of what true worship is. We quote lyrics with no intention of living them out. We raise our hands but haven't truly surrendered our lives. Worship should cost us something. When a landowner offered to give David a piece of property to build an altar on, David refused the handout. He insisted on paying for the land, saying, "I will not sacrifice to the LORD my God burnt offerings that cost me nothing" (2 Sam. 24:24). If you want to be a worshipper, let your work cost you something.

Christians should be the hardest workers at their jobs. Our work is worship. Paul wrote, "Whatever you do, work at it with all your heart, as working for the Lord, not for human masters" (Col. 3:23). We aren't working hard for human masters, but we are working hard for an eternal God who deserves our absolute best. When you go above and beyond what is expected, people begin to question your motives. When they ask you why you work so hard, you tell them about your true boss. Our job performance should point people to Jesus. Unfortunately that isn't true for many of us, but it is never too late to change. Starting today, bring your absolute best to your workplace. Remind yourself daily that you are doing things "as working for the Lord." If your paycheck is low, don't be frustrated. God will "meet all your needs according to the riches of his glory in Christ Jesus" (Phil. 4:19).

How would we work if Jesus was our boss? I know I would show up early. I wouldn't cut corners (mostly because he is God and would know it). I would give my all. I would be the best worker he has because my ultimate goal in life is to please God. This is how we should work for our earthly masters.

Let me reemphasize this one point: your hard work could be one of your greatest witnesses to the lost world. It was my hard work as a McDonald's employee that opened the door for me to speak into the lives of my coworkers. They admired who I was behind the scenes, and it gave me an inroad to introduce them to Jesus. I was working for Jesus in an indirect way through my earthly manager at McDonald's. She wasn't a believer, but she was my assignment. I took ownership of showing her how a Christian should work.

I would intentionally stay late so I could get some conversations in with her about faith. She eventually came to church with me and surrendered her life to Christ. It was my first big "win" as a follower of Jesus. What sold her on it? I didn't have the right words to say, but I did have the right actions to show her.

You might be the only Bible someone will ever read. You might be the only version of Jesus people ever experience. When someone says "Christian," they will associate your life with that title. Let your worth ethic be a bridge that gets them to Jesus, not a barrier that keeps them from the faith.

When our work becomes an act of worship, the response from God is a blessing. He sees the excellence and opens doors no man can open. Jesus taught this principle, saying, "Give, and it will be given to you. A good measure, pressed down, shaken together and running over, will be poured into your lap. For with the measure you use, it will be measured to you" (Luke 6:38). This is mostly used to encourage generosity, but the context is bigger than money. It is about how you use your life. When you exert energy toward hard work, God sees it and will reward you.

THE UNFAIR ADVANTAGE: WORK HARD

It was Joseph's work ethic, not his prayer life, that set him up for promotion. Prayer is crucially important, but if you want to be set apart, you have to work hard. I want to drive this home: the more unfair the situation, the harder you should work. If you feel like they are taking advantage of you, work hard. If you feel underpaid, work hard. If you feel like you got skipped over for the promotion, work hard. I'm pretty sure you have never been sold into slavery, but you might have done an internship where you weren't paid, you might have taken a lower salary than you wanted, or you might have been demoted because of a financial crisis. Life is full of unfair work situations. Joseph showed that no matter the situation, we are called to work hard.

During the 2008 financial crisis, our church took a big hit. My pastor had to make some decisions that would affect people's employment. My friend Paul ran our middle school group and unfortunately was on the list for a financial demotion. His pay was cut by 60 percent. I remember thinking, *Paul is going to quit.* But Paul didn't quit. He did the opposite: he worked harder. It was unfair that he was doing more work for less pay. But Paul knew the principles I am teaching in this chapter. The more unfair the situation, the harder you should work.

Paul's pay was restored a year or so later. But that is only a fraction of the story. Paul eventually transitioned off that staff and pursued a calling as a full-time evangelist. His hard work ethic helped him launch an incredible ministry that has seen over two hundred thousand decisions for Christ. This is unreal! Paul is reaping the benefits of hard work during an unfair season. Seeing two hundred thousand decisions for Christ is impressive, but so was Paul's decision to work hard even when he wasn't getting paid for the work he was doing. No wonder God is blessing his ministry.

Everyone wants great opportunities, but few are willing to embrace a great work ethic. Everyone wants honor, but few want to hustle. Do you want God's grace on your life? Start grinding. Work hard at what God has given you. Joseph was promoted. Why? Because his boss saw that something was different about him. Potiphar acknowledged that "the LORD was with him and that the LORD gave him success in everything he did" (Gen. 39:3). Can your employer see Jesus in your work ethic? Can your supervisor see Jesus in your attitude? Can they see Jesus in your excellence?

Don't wait for the dream job. Start now. You feel underpaid, overlooked, and insignificant? God is watching. It might be unfair, but in the right time you will be promoted. It will start with a small promotion in Potiphar's house, but eventually it will lead to a large promotion as second-in-command over all of Egypt. The sky is the limit when our work is done "unto the Lord."

DISCUSSION QUESTIONS

Hard work is an intentional commitment even when we feel undervalued. Many times we let the circumstances dictate our work instead of our work being worship unto God. Take a few minutes to answer these questions about your work ethic.

1. What healthy and unhealthy model(s) of work ethic have you experienced?
2. How would you describe your current work ethic?
3. What keeps you from giving your absolute best work to your current situation?
4. How can you remind yourself that your work is worship?
5. What can you change today to make worship cost you something?

UNFAIR ADVANTAGE #4

THE SEDUCED
SAINT

After a while his master's wife took notice of
Joseph and said, "Come to bed with me!"

GENESIS 39:7

A few decades ago, I heard a sermon by theologian Dr. Michael Brown that changed my life. It influenced me so greatly that I have been teaching its concept ever since. The original message described a Hebrew word that is found repeatedly in the book of Proverbs. This word, _acharit_ (pronounced ah-kha-reet), is defined as "that which comes after" or "the final end."[1]

Every decision, every situation, and every life has an acharit. The problem is that it is often ignored in favor of

86

the present moment. In other words, the Enemy shows us the bait and never reveals the hook. The acharit, the final consequence, is hidden. It reminds me of the movie *The Sixth Sense*. If you have seen it, then you know the ending is a shocker. No one could have expected it. Many people, after watching the movie for the first time, go back and watch it again trying to find any clues that may hint at such a crazy ending. I won't give it away, but let's just say things are not as they appear.

When you know the end, you look at the rest differently. The Enemy's goal is to blind you from the acharit. If sin is enticing enough, then the end result will be completely forgotten. I believe if we could only look ahead to the guilt and the shame of our choices, then we would avoid sin at all cost. In other words, if we kept the acharit in mind, we would never play around with sin.

Proverbs tells us, "Listen to advice and accept discipline, and at the end [acharit] you will be counted among the wise" (Prov. 19:20). I want my children and grandchildren to experience the end results of my life lived with integrity, and not the shame of my sinful past. How is this possible? We must continuously remember sin always has consequences.

At the time of writing this, our world is being rocked because of the scandals of Ravi Zacharias. Ravi was one of the greatest apologists of our time. Before this, if you needed any help defending your faith, his books and sermons were the go-to resources. He helped an entire generation grow closer to Jesus. I watched Ravi's funeral in May of 2020. Vice President Mike Pence attended. It was a beautiful tribute to more than forty years of ministry. Every pastor and church leader was inspired to finish well like Ravi did. Or so we thought.

Months after Ravi's death, the board of Ravi Zacharias International Ministries (RZIM) started an investigation into sexual abuse allegations coming from multiple women that reportedly occurred at different massage parlors. After a thorough investigation, the charges held up and Ravi's name, influence, and legacy instantly fell apart. My heart hurts for the women terribly victimized by a man who should have been an example of faith to them. My heart also hurts for his children and grandchildren, who will now live with the stain of his sin rather than a Christlike legacy to be proud of. I truly believe that if Ravi could have seen these final consequences of his dark sin, he never would have given in to the destructive pull of his temptations.

Many people have lost their health, families, jobs, ministries, freedom, and influence because they focused on the moment of pleasure (the bait) while never considering the consequences (the hook). Use this book as a warning to never give in to anything you wouldn't be okay with having broadcast on the news. I tell my staff my goal is never to be in the newspaper, unless I am the one who took out the advertisement.

The principle of the acharit also works in the positive. Billy Graham passed away a few years ago at ninety-nine years old. As of 2008, Graham's estimated lifetime audience, including radio and television broadcasts, topped 2.2 billion.[2] Billy Graham was known not only for his powerful preaching but also for a lifetime of consistently good character. His funeral was viewed by millions around the world, and his legacy lives on in his children and grandchildren. So many aspects of his life have become the gold standard for ministry.

I have to believe that Billy Graham was always thinking with the end in mind. He envisioned his acharit and maintained his purity despite all the temptations of the world. Even more than building a legacy for his grandchildren, he, like Moses as recorded in the book of Hebrews, was "looking ahead to his reward" (Heb. 11:26).

The acharit comes into play in our story of Joseph as well. After the unexpected twist of Joseph's promotion at Potiphar's house, he began to thrive in his new role. Then, out of nowhere, Joseph has a crisis. It was not a crisis with his calling. It was not a crisis with his community. It was a crisis with his character. Everyone's character will eventually be tested. Sadly, many people have the charisma to take them to the top, but they do not have the character to keep them there.

Joseph's test of character came just after his promotion. This is a common strategy of the Enemy. He waits for you to be at your prime before he tries to plunder you. The passage tells us that "Joseph was well-built and handsome" (Gen. 39:6), a burden I also have had to carry most of my life. I am totally joking. But I do find it interesting the Scriptures mention this phrase. Other versions say "favored," but when you look up the original Hebrew, it is clear he was a good-looking guy.

Joseph's looks were so remarkable that "after a while his master's wife took notice of Joseph" (Gen. 39:7). This was getting awkward. Joseph was trying to make the most of his season, to be faithful in serving Potiphar, but then came temptation. There are few desires as strong as sexual temptations.

She trapped Joseph when he was alone and said, "Come to bed with me!" In the face of choosing temporary pleasure or lasting integrity, Joseph stood his ground and made the choice to refuse her advances. So she stepped it up. Scripture reports that on another occasion, "She caught him by his cloak and said, 'Come to bed with me!' But he left his cloak in her hand and ran out of the house" (Gen. 39:12). This guy has the worst luck with cloaks! One cloak almost got him killed by his brothers, and the other one ended up being a tool in the hand of a vindictive woman.

Potiphar's wife was thirsty. Joseph could have given in and would have possibly experienced some momentary advantages for it. It would have satisfied his young sexual appetite and given him an alliance with the woman of the house. It might have been a win-win. The bait was within reach and enticing, but what was unseen was the hook that always lies near. Sin is costly. Giving up your character is detrimental.

In one way or another, we have all been in similar situations. No, I have never been assaulted by my boss's wife, but I have had moments where my character was put to the test. Joseph's story is an extreme example, and I think guarding our integrity is less about the big moments and more about the small moments we face every single day.

Consider what may have gone through Joseph's head. Sex possibly could have helped him in the short-term. A hidden affair with Potiphar's wife may have granted him privileges no one else would have gotten. The Bible tells us that sin is pleasurable, for a season (Heb. 11:25). Sin is easy to get into. Integrity is hard to keep. But Joseph "left his cloak in her hand and ran out of the house." This is strong language. He ran away from sin. In a culture where so many are running toward sin, God is looking for people who will run as far away from it as possible. Joseph chose to maintain his integrity. Considering the fleeting benefits that sin can offer, to run away from it may seem unfair, especially when it seems like everyone else is enjoying it consequence-free. Keep running, though, because it is for your advantage.

Joseph's decision was quick and most likely predetermined. In the heat of the moment, pleasure is difficult to resist, so it can be assumed he had committed himself before this moment to stay pure and faithful to the Lord. Joseph chose not to give in to temporary satisfaction and instead exchanged it for short-term pain. It is painful to stay sexually pure. It is painful not to cheat on your taxes. It is painful to keep your word. Maintaining your integrity is painful. But it produces a life where you can say, "I have fought the good fight, I have finished the race, I have kept the faith. Now there is in store for me the crown of righteousness" (2 Tim. 4:7–8).

YOUR MOST IMPORTANT ASSET

Integrity is a missing value in our society. Integrity is doing what is right when no one else is looking. It comes from the same Latin root as *integer*, which is a whole number. To be a person of integrity means you are a person of wholeness. You are the real deal in the spotlight and the real deal behind the scenes.

Our world is in desperate need of men and women to be the real deal. People are more skeptical than ever of Christians, and especially of Christian leaders. As I am writing this, the last year has exposed multiple high-profile Christian leaders as frauds. Scandal has shaken up the church, and we need to reprioritize the value of our integrity.

It may feel unfair that you can't do whatever pleases you at that very moment. It may feel unfair that you can't lie, cheat, or sleep your way to the top. It may feel unfair that you can't relax to the same pleasures other people enjoy. It may feel unfair that the right road is so much more difficult to take than the wrong road.

A life of integrity is your greatest advantage.

It's unfair!

But as you will see throughout this chapter, maintaining your integrity might just be the greatest advantage toward your future. A life of integrity is your greatest advantage, but a lack of integrity is your great disqualifier.

People do not need a motto to say; they need a model to follow. Paul challenged those following him to model what he did: "Whatever you have learned or received or heard from me, or seen in me—put it into practice" (Phil. 4:9). Paul went further to say, "Follow my example, as I follow the example of Christ" (1 Cor. 11:1).

What is the stupidest piece of advice ever given? "Do as I say, not as I do." People do not follow our words; they follow our actions. For example, a study evaluating teens who smoke cigarettes showed that 92 percent of them had parents who also smoked.[3] Why? People do not care what you say, they care what you do.

John Maxwell discusses the importance of integrity in his book *Developing the Leader Within You*. He says, "Eighty-nine percent of what people learn comes through visual stimulation, 10 percent through audible stimulation, and 1 percent through other senses. So it makes sense that the more followers see and hear their leader being consistent in action and word, the greater their consistency and loyalty. *What they hear, they understand. What they see, they believe!*"[4]

Currently the world is seeing Christ's church continuing to suffer from a lack of integrity. The church world is being sucker punched by leaders who give in to temptation and tragically fall morally. It has become so common that it is no longer shocking, but it has to bring so much grief to the heart of God.

My parents' lives were transformed in the 1980s in Baton Rouge under the ministry of Jimmy Swaggart. In the '70s and '80s Jimmy Swaggart had the largest tele-vision ministry in the world. In 1987, his ministry had a combined income of $150 million. That is equivalent to $393.5 million in 2023.[5] There is no ministry that com-pares to it today. But integrity matters, and sadly Jimmy Swaggart went through one of the most public unravelings of his integrity. I don't need to spend time spelling out his struggles, but his fall was deep and a lot of people were hurt because of it.

As great as Jimmy Swaggart's ministry was, without integrity it collapsed. The once thriving Bible college has been sold off to the city and is now being used for government offices. Although he has since repented and done good work for God, his Wikipedia page has been forever written. God forgives and forgets; people don't.

The point of the story is this: integrity matters. Your talent can take you to the top, but it is integrity that will keep you there. It takes a long time to climb the mountain of influence but only a second to fall all the way to the bottom. I want to give you some tips over the next few sections on maintaining your integrity. My biggest concern is not the influence I may obtain but the influence I would lose if my character can't keep up with my calling. Integrity is the glue that holds your influence intact.

DON'T BE A HYPOCRITE

Hypocrisy is the act of saying one thing but doing another. It is frowned upon by everyone but practiced by pretty much everyone as well. We all say one thing and find ourselves doing another. This is human nature. I once shared on a podcast how I wake up every day at 5 a.m. The truth is that I wake up five to six days a week at 5 a.m. Having moments where you do not live up exactly to what you say is common. Slipping up once in a while can be understood, but being an outright hypocrite is *not* okay.

Being a hypocrite is different than showing occasional hypocrisy. A hypocrite is a person who intentionally deceives you to believe something about them, but truthfully they are something very different. When found out, a hypocrite loses much, including the respect of the world around them.

The word *hypocrite* ultimately came into English from the Greek word *hypokrites*, which means "an actor" or "a stage player."[6] The actors in the ancient Greek world would wear large masks on stage. The idea was that if you wore a mask, you were a hypocrite. Another way of saying it is that you have two faces. You have the face you show, and then you have the real you underneath. This is why moral failures are so devastating for the church. The world looks in and presumes the people onstage are actors. They are putting on a face in the front of the church and then they have a secret life behind the scenes. When scandals come to light, it just confirms what the skeptic already thought about religious people.

How do we confront this issue? No one, not even leaders, can be perfect. There has been only one perfect leader on earth and he died, rose again, and then ascended to heaven two thousand years ago. There are only imperfect people and imperfect leaders. Our goal is not to impress with false perfection but to impact with honest transparency. I have issues. I struggle. My church hears my honesty in these phrases also. I struggle because I am human. I am a preacher because God has called and gifted me for it, but I struggle with sin because I am a human living in a fallen world.

SECRET VS. PRIVATE

I have a theory that most people can handle everything except for secrecy. A scandal occurs not because the person had a struggle but because they had a secret. Secrets sell books, they become blockbuster movies, and they even hold governments together. Secrets are the scandals everyone is looking for. So how do we handle this secret-starved society? We provide no secrets to be discovered. We live as an open book, having nothing to hide.

My goal is to have no secrets; however, I do have things that are private. For instance, if you come to my house, there are no secrets. We have nothing sinister or scandalous hidden in our home, but we do have rooms that are private. If you strolled into my master bedroom and started looking around, that would be very weird. That's a personal area that is not open for everyone. There are no secrets, but there is privacy. People have a right to privacy, but Christians do not have a right to secrecy.

From the very beginning, man has been trying to hide. When Adam sinned, his immediate go-to was secrecy. When God called out to him, Adam answered, "I heard you in the garden, and I was afraid because I was naked; so I hid" (Gen. 3:10). Then God asked him the best question: "Who told you that you were naked?" (Gen. 3:11). I admit that I have had this nightmare. In it, I am preaching and I look down and, yep, I'm totally naked. I guess I just forgot to put on clothes before church. It is always such a relief to wake up and realize this was just a dream and will never happen in real life because I think it's safe to say that I will always remember to put my clothes on. The point is that no one just randomly figures out they are naked.

What happened to Adam and Eve? They sinned and instead of running to God, they ran from God in their shame. They tried to hide their issues. They assumed they would be safe behind their secrecy. They tried to excuse it as privacy. But the truth is, they never had to cover that issue before. It became a problem only when sin and shame became involved.

In 1997, I was in seventh grade and a classmate was talking to a group of friends about how he wanted to see the newest movie, *L.A. Confidential.* I have no clue why I did this, but I walked over and told the group I had seen the movie. I hadn't. I wasn't even allowed to watch R-rated movies, and to be honest, I still never have seen this movie.

The group gravitated around me like I was a guru with infinite wisdom to offer. They asked me what it was about, and off I went. I never knew I was so creative in coming up with a movie plot right off the top of my head. I rambled for a while about how a CIA agent knew of a bomb plot in California. He had to go back in a time machine to stop a chain of events that would lead to the eventual destruction of Los Angeles. I am sure if you actually saw *L.A. Confidential,* this is a whole lot more humorous.

I kept up this lie for weeks. It was exhausting. People wouldn't let it go that I had seen such a grown-up movie, and they wanted my insight. So I kept making stuff up. I remember thinking I had better write down my plot, so I didn't forget anything I'd said! Eventually my friends found out I was lying. You can only keep up the act for so long.

This is how secrecy works. It becomes your full-time job to hold up a house of cards that will eventually crash down.

The solution to the problem of secrecy is openness. We need to be vulnerable with the secret things in our lives. Do you struggle with substance abuse? Pornography? Gambling? Hatred? Pride? Or something else? Don't hide behind the secrecy of these. Secrets are always exposed one way or another. As hard as it is, tell someone now. Getting honest is the first step to getting healthy. Remember, some things are still private. So every detail does not always need to be shared, and some people are not equipped to handle your struggles. Use wisdom but share your secret with someone trustworthy. It is a good first step to freedom.

One of the lost arts in Christian community is confession. The Catholic Church has a history of making healthy church disciplines into strict church laws. Because confession got weird, people missed the point of how powerful it is to share our secrets with one another. The book of James tells us, "Therefore confess your sins to each other and pray for each other so that you may be healed. The prayer of a righteous person is powerful and effective" (James 5:16). Jesus alone forgives. We do not find forgiveness from people. But we do find healing when we confess one to another. Do you have a trusted friend or pastor you can share your secrets with? You will begin your journey to freedom as soon as you move past your confinement and into confession.

You have two choices with your secrets: expose them or be exposed. Jesus tells us, "For all that is secret will eventually be brought into the open, and everything that is concealed will be brought to light and made known to all" (Luke 8:17 NLT). When you humbly reveal your issues, people can have grace to help you move on and find freedom. However, when you are discovered, people feel deceived, and the fall is much harder.

CHUTES AND LADDERS

When I think of integrity, I am reminded of the game Chutes and Ladders. My family played lots of board games when I was growing up, and I have tried to keep the tradition alive with my five kids. My goal is to beat them in every game for as long as possible. No mercy. Life is tough and losing at Life and Monopoly should help them see this, but that is a lesson for another day.

Chutes and Ladders is a board game with squares numbered from one to one hundred. Obviously, you start at one and the goal is to make it to one hundred first. Like life, it is a race to the top. Also like life, there are ladders that are available along the way. A ladder can take you a couple of spaces ahead or even a few rows ahead.

We have all experienced ladders in life. A coach believed in you and gave you a cool opportunity. You inherited some money from a grandparent or you married rich. You experienced God's grace and got a position you never deserved. We've all had moments that, looking back, we realize took us further faster than we could have ever thought. Life is filled with ladders.

The game is also filled with chutes. A chute is a slide

that can take you back either a few spots or, if you're really unlucky, all the way to the bottom. Life is filled with chutes. Sometimes the chute is outside of your control: a job loss, a health diagnosis, a rejection letter. Chutes come in all shapes and sizes, but arguably the most aggressive chute would be a lapse in character. Moral failures in a marriage, a company, a church, and even in a friendship can take you from the top of the game to the bottom in a matter of seconds.

Pray for God to send you ladders. But also pray that you would avoid any chutes along the way. Jesus told us to pray, "Lead us not into temptation, but deliver us from the evil one" (Matt. 6:13). To paraphrase this prayer according to our illustration, we could say, "Protect me from these chutes the devil is putting along my path." I pray this often. Joseph must have prayed it also. He avoided a massive chute that would have tanked his potential.

There is a long list of people who have been given incredible ladders. These people did phenomenal things for God's kingdom. They climbed to the highest levels of Christian influence. But when it mattered most, they didn't avoid the tempting chute in their path, and they were quickly thrown to the bottom. I do not say this to scare you, but I do write this to warn you. Do not add your name to that list. Stay humble. Stay accountable. Stay teachable. Stay in prayer and ask God to guard your integrity. Integrity doesn't build the dream

> When integrity is a nonnegotiable, a house of cards becomes a house of concrete.

fast, but it does build the dream firm. When integrity is a nonnegotiable, a house of cards becomes a house of concrete.

REMEMBER UNCLE ESAU

Do you remember Esau in the Bible? Esau was the twin brother of Joseph's father, Jacob. Their conflict with each other began even before birth when these two boys wrestled within their mother's womb. Esau won by coming out first (although Jacob was grabbing his heel on the way out, indicating the fight wasn't over yet). So Esau was the firstborn and out of tradition he was the heir to the birthright. This made him the next head of the home. He would receive a double portion of the family's significant inheritance and would be responsible for the estate when his father died. It was an incredible honor and responsibility to have the birthright.

As the Bible begins to describe Jacob and Esau, it is easier to envision Esau as the manlier of the two. In modern times, I picture Esau shopping at Bass Pro and Jacob shopping at Target. In the biblical story, one day Esau came in from a long day of hunting to find Jacob home cooking a stew. Scripture tells us, "Esau came in from the open country, famished" (Gen. 25:29). That word "famished" is translated in other versions as "faint," "hungry," and "starving."

We do stupid things when we are hungry. Our physical, emotional, and sexual hunger drives us to make decisions we would never make in a normal setting. This is why you do not go grocery shopping while you are hungry.

Everything looks good, and the diet and the budget quickly go out the window. A recent study from the University of Dundee surveyed fifty people in two different scenarios, once while they were hungry and once while they were full. Results showed that "hunger 'significantly' altered people's decision-making."[7] People make bad choices when they are driven by hunger. The study went on to show the significance of hunger on the ability to wait or expect immediate gratification. "If you offered people a reward now or doubled the reward in the future, they were normally willing to wait for 35 days to double the reward, but when hungry, this fell to three days."[8]

Much like the people in this study, Esau was hungry, desperate, and vulnerable. So when he asked his brother for some stew, Jacob saw his chance. He connivingly said, "First sell me your birthright" (Gen. 25:31). *What?* That makes zero sense. Jacob wanted to exchange Esau's lofty inheritance for a little bowl of stew? Shockingly, though, immediate gratification won out and Esau gave in. "Look, I am about to die," Esau said. "What good is the birthright to me?" (Gen. 25:32). He wasn't going to die. We can all miss a meal or two, or ten. But this is how sin operates.

Sin exchanges what we want most with what we want now. There is no way that Esau's greatest desire was to have stew. His future rested on his birthright. It was his destiny. But Esau gave up what he wanted most, his birthright, for what he wanted now, stew. Sound stupid? We often do the same thing.

Good jobs, beautiful families, solid ministries, and personal health are common prices paid in exchange for the destructive indulgences of affairs, addictions, short-term pleasures, and instant gratifications. These things have wrecked the lives and futures of many people. What are you hungry for? Sex? Influence? Attention? Money? Prestige? So many Christians give up what they want most for what they want now. They want sex now. They want gratification now. They want security now. In the words of Veruca Salt in *Willy Wonka and the Chocolate Factory*, "I don't care how, I want it now."[9]

Esau made the worst deal in history, and even though his story has continued to be told thousands of years later, people still have not learned from it. Short-term desire is not worth your long-term dream.

Joseph didn't make the same kind of hasty decision, though. He must have known the old story of his father's deceptively earned birthright. So in moments of "hunger," I like to think the poor choice of Uncle Esau frequently came to mind. I wonder if in a moment of temptation with Potiphar's wife, he was thinking of his uncle's rash choice as a warning. It was the kind of personal story he needed to clear his mind.

Learning from the failures of others is a great way to keep your own integrity. You always have a choice to make. Learning from someone else's failure can be the image to hold on to so you avoid a slip in moments of desperation. Perhaps Joseph learned from his Uncle Esau. He imagined the pain that Esau must have felt. The pain of regret. I experience this each time I hear of another person's fall. My heart always goes out to the family and any others who were hurt. I hate that so many lives can be damaged so quickly. I know I never want to find myself in that situation.

The temporary satisfaction is not worth it. Doing things the hard way can feel very unfair. It is unfair that it will take you longer because you do not cut corners. It is unfair you can't have all the "fun" your friends are having. But integrity is for your advantage. It is the moments of private integrity that bring the long-term gain.

BOOGER IN YOUR NOSE

We have all had it happen. Unfortunately, it is an occurrence that seems only to happen when lots of people are present. It could be after an extended coffee break with friends, or after talking to numerous people in the church lobby, or immediately following an important business meeting where you were the presenter. Whatever the environment, the horror is always the same. A quick glimpse at your reflection shows a booger in plain sight. The internal questions come in a flood. *How long has it been there? Was it there the whole time? Did this person see? What about that person? When was the last time I looked in the mirror so I can have some kind of time frame?* And the most important question: *Why did no one say anything?*

If you have ever been the person on the other side of the scenario, then you know the answer to the last one. It's just awkward! It's embarrassing to the person to bring it up, and it's definitely embarrassing to the person it has happened to. And it is not always a booger. Sometimes it's spinach in your teeth or a shirt on backward. It's things that are in plain sight to everyone, except for the culprit. Everyone can see it, but to avoid embarrassment, no one says anything. But I just want to set the record straight. Tell me! You know what's more embarrassing than saying something? A booger hanging outside of my nose.

We don't know what we don't know. We all have blind spots, areas where our view is obstructed. If you see something, you should say something. This is the rule that I believe every healthy community lives by. If I see something, I will say something. If I see someone doing a good job, I will give them a shout-out. If I see something that needs to get fixed, I will say something. If I see a possible red flag in someone's character, I will say something.

Years ago, I ran an internship program for young leaders in training for ministry. These young men and women are still some of my favorite people on the planet. We would travel all over the world together doing ministry trips and always laughing together. On one trip we were ministering at a church in New Orleans and decided to spend a free day hanging out in the city, around the French Quarter.

We got one of my favorite American classics for lunch, Subway. Standing in line to order, I heard one of my young guys order water to drink, which both surprised and impressed me. In the long time I had known him, I don't think I had ever seen him drink anything other than soda and milkshakes. Wow! I was glad he was turning over a new leaf.

Things took an ugly turn, though, when we walked to the drink station and, as bold as can be, he pressed that plastic water cup against that gray lever and filled it with ice-cold Pepsi. I just looked at him in shock. He had no clue that what he was doing was wrong. And when I asked him what he was doing, he casually told me he was getting his drink and then he would find us a table. He didn't know what he didn't know.

Part of good mentoring or good parenting is finding ways to make life lessons unforgettable. I am not great at this. But I am learning. So on this hot summer day in New Orleans, I knew I had to seize the moment. I pulled him aside, asking him why he thought it was okay to take something he didn't pay for. My flesh wanted to say, "At least put Sprite in it; you aren't fooling anyone with the Pepsi."

His response was typical, something along the lines of: These drinks don't even cost money for the company. It's ridiculous to pay $1.50 for a soda. Everyone he knows orders water but gets soda. It was how he had always done it . . .

But culture does not dictate our character. Scripture does. As Christians our character is valuable—in this case, worth far more than a soda. Character blind spots happen to all of us, and it's necessary to have people in our lives to call them out. This lesson spurred my young friend to go back to pay for his drink. It was a small moment that prayerfully produced a more Christlike character.

The apostle Paul challenged us to "carry each other's burdens, and in this way you will fulfill the law of Christ" (Gal. 6:2). One way that we carry others' burdens is by pointing out future pitfalls in a kind and grace-filled way. Paul went on to say, "If anyone thinks they are something when they are not, they deceive themselves" (Gal. 6:3). We are far more deceived than we know in thinking we are doing the right thing, and we need one another to point out the fault.

It's important to surround ourselves with people who tell us what we need to hear, even if it's not necessarily what we want to hear. I am not looking for shallow praise, I am looking for lasting progress. Help me identify the booger in my nose.

There is something you do that you do not know you do, that everyone else knows you do. Read that sentence again, because realizing this could change your life. You have a blind spot everyone can see—except you. To discover this, you have to seek out feedback. Ask the people who know you best what yours might be.

I was traveling with a pastor friend, and we were sitting in the hotel room just talking between sessions. He innocently brought up a joke that was made about me by some other pastors. They were all making fun of one hand gesture they said I did too often. At first, I was offended. My feelings got hurt. But after I thought about it, I was glad my friend said something. After watching videos, I saw the hand movement I had never noticed before. It looked ridiculous.

Patrick Lencioni's book *The Ideal Team Player* really helped shape this idea for me and for our staff culture. He said every ideal team member is humble, hungry, and smart.[10] (Side note: Is it just me or does it bother anyone else that the third word doesn't also start with *H*?)

In the book, the word "smart" doesn't refer to IQ but

to a person's ability to interact with people. It is the skill of not being awkward, as well as being able to read a room. When improving "people smarts," Lencioni's advice is that you have to have a healthy feedback culture. People need to have the ability to speak into our awkwardness and bring correction.

A healthy community not only celebrates but also corrects. It is filled with both grace and truth. Sometimes we may be on the receiving end of feedback, and sometimes we will have the responsibility to give it. When giving it, let me guide you on how to best point out the blind spots in others.

First, correct in love. What is your motivation? If it is to shame or nitpick them, don't say anything. Love should drive everything we do. If you love me, you will truly want me to get better. A strategic way of correcting in love is what we call the "sandwich method." You start with love and grace. You tell them some things they are doing really well. Next you introduce what could be made better—this is the middle of the sandwich—and then you close with how awesome they are. Surround the correction in an attitude of love. Approach is everything. You can have the right content but the wrong approach, and the situation will turn out wrong. Approach in love.

Second, correct in private. When correction is done in public, the outcome is shame and a divide in the relationship. When correction is done privately, the outcome is change and a deepening in the relationship. Something I always live by is to praise in public and rebuke in private. That phrase is foundational to a culture of honor.

Third, correct it, then forget it. In other words, move on. The best demonstrator of this is Jesus. "I will forgive their wickedness and will remember their sins no more" (Heb. 8:12). So if you correct me, I will receive it, but please don't bring it up again. You don't have to keep reminding me of the booger you found. Move on and let that moment of correction be a part of the past.

If you work on my team, my goal is to make you better. I care about your feelings, but I care more about your future. It would do a disservice to ignore your blind spots that may limit your future. Friends and family members can see pits ahead of you that you don't recognize yet. "The way of a fool is right in his own eyes, but a wise man listens to advice" (Prov. 12:15 ESV). Whom do you allow to speak into your life? Who is telling you what you need to hear, not just what you want to hear? Your integrity is about not just the obvious sins but also the blind spots those closest to you can notice.

I bought a new SUV last year that has a blind spot alert. When I start to go into another lane that has a car or obstacle in my blind spot, the alert starts beeping: *beep, beep, beep.* This is what healthy community does for you. They help you recognize your drift into disaster. "As iron sharpens iron, so one person sharpens another" (Prov. 27:17). Do you have those friends? If not, seek them out. Get involved in a small group at your church. Connect with a serve team. Enroll in a Bible study. If you don't have good friends, be a good friend. Ask God to bring those people into your life, and you will be shocked at how he answers that request.

INTEGRITY FOR OUR ADVANTAGE

Dr. Billy Graham said, "Integrity is the glue that holds our way of life together. We must constantly strive to keep our integrity intact. When wealth is lost, nothing is lost; when health is lost, something is lost; when character is lost, all is lost."[11] I urge you: Don't lose your integrity. Hold on to it.

A few years back Katie and I went on an anniversary cruise to Alaska. It was one of our favorite cruises. At one point we were enjoying the scenery from the ship, when off the balcony I saw an iceberg. Now, I saw the movie *Titanic* enough times to know that an iceberg is the last thing I want to see out in open water. For a second I thought about warning someone in the captain's quarter, but then common sense returned, and I was sure that the cruise industry wouldn't make that mistake twice.

An iceberg is a broken-off piece of a glacier. They range anywhere from six feet wide to the largest on record, 183 miles wide. Icebergs are remarkable because only a fraction of the ice is shown above the waterline. This was the issue with the *Titanic*. It wasn't what was visible that sank the ship. It was all that was under the surface.

Integrity is who you are below the surface. It can be easy to become very focused only on the part of ourselves that everyone can see. Sometimes we even try to make excuses by saying, "If no one knows, then it doesn't matter." But integrity always matters. And what is below the surface can be the thing that either sinks your ship or keeps you afloat. If we concentrate on maintaining our hidden integrity, our visible reputation will take care of itself.

Building integrity is possible, but it requires deep evaluation of what is going on below the surface. At our church we often bring our leadership through an evaluation to get an idea of their level of integrity. Here are just a few of the questions:

- How well do I treat people from whom I can gain nothing?
- Am I the same person alone as I am when I'm in the spotlight?
- Do I freely admit my faults without being pressed?
- Do I esteem others better then myself and routinely put them first in all of my actions and decisions?
- Do I always hold to the same moral standards, or do circumstances determine my choices?
- Do I make difficult decisions, even when they may cost me something?
- When I have a problem with somebody, do I talk to them or about them?
- Would I be ashamed if people could know the imagination and thoughts that I entertain?
- What would I do if I knew I would never be found out or be punished for it?
- Are my actions governed more out of concern for my reputation or out of genuine love for God and my neighbor?

These honest evaluations reveal areas where we may need to humbly go to the Lord in prayer. We all have character flaws, but we also have a God who is quick to help.

Have you already screwed up? God specializes in redemption. In the Bible, King David sinned greatly when he called Bathsheba to his palace to sleep with him. Then he continued his vicious cycle by attempting to cover this sin by ordering her husband to be killed. As extreme as this example is, we often also try to sweep our issues under the rug. Here is a notification for you: "Be sure that your sin will find you out" (Num. 32:23).

When David was confronted by a prophet, he didn't take Adam and Eve's approach and hide. He repented and ran toward the Lord. He prayed out, "Have mercy on me, O God, according to your unfailing love; according to your great compassion blot out my transgressions. Wash away all my iniquity and cleanse me from my sin" (Ps. 51:1–2). Repentance is a turning from our sin and toward God's forgiveness. It is never too late to receive God's grace. Have you messed up? God is willing and able to forgive you and give you a fresh start.

Joseph chose his integrity, but even this choice was costly. Having integrity will often cost you some earthly fun, some friends, some conversations, and even some years in the spotlight. In Joseph's case it would be nice if the story of Potiphar's wife had ended differently. But even though he had integrity, she did not, and Joseph ended up being severely punished.

People will not always celebrate your integrity. Being a person of character is extremely honorable and it has immense lasting results, but it is not through the quick path that the world offers. Joseph's choice brought him from a promotion to prison. Our passage tells us, "Joseph's master took him and put him in prison, the place where the king's prisoners were confined" (Gen. 39:20).

We are in a culture that celebrates immediate gratification. The choice to guard your integrity is a long play. It might lead you down before it leads you up. It might slow you down before you speed up. You might be misjudged before you are ministering to the masses.

It is unfair that Joseph was thrown into prison. It looked like a detour. It looked like wasted time, but nothing is wasted with God. If he is moving you, it is always toward your destiny: "The LORD makes firm the steps of the one who delights in him" (Ps. 37:23). If you do the right thing, you can trust that God is directing your steps, even if those steps don't make sense at first.

DISCUSSION QUESTIONS

Integrity is your most important asset. In the same way we go to the doctor for regular checkups, we should also go to the Lord and a trusted friend for a regular character checkup. Spend a few minutes answering these questions.

1. How has a lapse in character by a friend, family member, or leader affected your life?
2. What blind spots have been revealed to you in the past?
3. Whom do you have in your life right now that can identify the "booger in your nose"?

4. When is the last time you got alone with God and asked him to reveal your flaws?
5. How can you make confession a regular spiritual discipline that you practice?

THE OPPRESSED OPPORTUNIST

When Joseph came to them the next morning, he saw that they were dejected. So he asked Pharaoh's officials who were in custody with him in his master's house, "Why do you look so sad today?" "We both had dreams," they answered, "but there is no one to interpret them." Then Joseph said to them, "Do not interpretations belong to God? Tell me your dreams."

GENESIS 40:6-8

A decade or so ago, *The Guardian* **put out a list of popular** books that had been written while the author was in prison. It was shocking to consider this list of world-renowned books that have sold millions of copies but were written during such dark and depressing times for their authors. *Don Quixote*, one of the world's most famous and widely translated books, was conceived and written as Miguel de Cervantes was serving multiple prison sentences. While his body was in prison, his mind was creating a masterpiece.

My favorite book on this list was written while the author was imprisoned for over a decade in an English jail cell in the city of Bedford. John Bunyan wrote arguably the most valuable and world-changing Christian work outside of the Bible. *The Pilgrim's Progress* is a classic. This past year I read the children's version to my kids, and it was as relevant and life-changing to this next generation as it has been for the past four hundred years.

The story of John Bunyan is fascinating. During the 1600s, any preaching outside of the state-run Church of England was banned. However, Bunyan, a Baptist minister, knew he was called to preach the Word of God, and even though he was warned to stop, he stood his ground and continued to take his message to as many people as he could. A warrant was issued for his arrest and still Bunyan didn't cower. He kept preaching until eventually he was arrested and began what would end up being a twelve-year prison sentence. The darkness of imprisonment was an obvious reality for him, but more people than Bunyan were impacted by his sentence. When his first wife died after their fourth child was born, Bunyan remarried, and his second wife, Elizabeth, was left alone to care for these children, one of whom was blind. Sadly, she gave birth to a stillborn child while Bunyan was in prison.

His family's sad situation was a tremendous burden on

Bunyan. He understood the pain he had inflicted on his family by standing for his faith. Bunyan wrote about his decision, "Oh! I saw in this condition I was as a man who was pulling down his house upon the head of his wife and children; yet thought I, I must do it, I must do it."[1] Despite his pain, his worry, and the hopelessness of his situation, Bunyan still found opportunities to express his faith while in his cell. One might say that during his oppression, he became an opportunist. In the darkness, the light of a new dream was birthed—a book that would leave a legacy for the next four centuries and counting. So the first section of the two-part bestselling novel, *The Pilgrim's Progress*, was envisioned and completed in the dark corners of a lonely jail cell.

After Bunyan was released from prison, his book was also released to the public, where it quickly sold over one hundred thousand copies. Bunyan suddenly became a famous and well-respected man. Now, not only was he able to care for his family once again, but he suddenly had significant opportunities to freely preach in places where thousands of people would come. His life and legacy were cemented because he made the most of his moments in prison.

In one way or another, dark moments happen to all of us. Each of us has faced difficult seasons where it seems impossible to find anything good. They all look different: the loss of a job, the death of a loved one, a bad diagnosis. No matter the issue, life is tough and often brings us to places of deep pain. This is where Joseph found himself in our story.

Amid perversion and power plays, Joseph made a valiant stance for purity. Where did this courage lead him? Straight to prison. Unfortunately, not all righteous decisions will lead to a shining palace. Faith is costly. Living for God sometimes lands us in the dungeons of life. You have been warned. Standing for what is right isn't always celebrated by man, but it is always celebrated by God. And if you don't stand for something, you will eventually fall for anything.

When I gave my life to Christ, I lost my four closest friends. They couldn't understand why I would choose church over partying, and so they left me without looking back. Being a sixteen-year-old whose life revolved around my social circle, I felt like this was the end of the world. I was alone and it was painful. It wasn't fair to be punished for something good. Perhaps this was a small glimpse of what Joseph felt, and an even smaller glimpse of what Christians all over the world feel who are being persecuted for their faith. It's never easy to walk through hardship. So what do we do when we find ourselves in a difficult place?

In a prison moment, people are left with two choices. They can lie down and weep, or they can lift their heads and work. Weep or work. Joseph became an opportunist in the middle of his oppression. I want to encourage you to make the most of your dark seasons as well. Our sufferings open opportunities that wouldn't be available in moments of ease. This is the unfair advantage. So buckle up. This chapter is going to challenge you to roll up your sleeves and seize the opportunities amid your oppression.

> Our sufferings open opportunities that wouldn't be available in moments of ease.

PURPOSE IN THE PRISON

Some believe the time span from the moment his brothers threw him into a pit until he found himself in an Egyptian prison was about one year. So it's probably safe to say Joseph had his worst year ever. He was probably only around nineteen years old, and his life was a continuous cycle of defeat after defeat. The next decade of his life, the prime of his twenties, would be spent locked up in a prison for a crime he never committed. You think *your* twenties were wasted? At least you got a few credits done at the community college. Joseph spent some of his best years in prison. The question is, why?

Why does God allow some of our prime, best years to be spent in private? I had so much more energy when I was twenty-two than I do in my late thirties. But I did not have near the opportunities when I was twenty-two. Maybe God knew something about the prison was necessary for Joseph. Get ready; this is about to get interesting.

The Egyptian culture of Joseph's time was always ahead of the game. Just a glimpse of the pyramids and you can easily see how advanced they were as a civilization. (Unless you believe aliens built them, and I actually know people who have tried to prove that to me.) Egyptians not only were advanced in architecture, education, and science, but also in how they ran their criminal justice system.

Prisons weren't a normal part of the ancient culture. The Old Testament has very few references to prisons or extended jail sentences. If you did something wrong, the punishment was usually getting beaten or killed. Egypt was one of the few societies that had a legitimate justice and prison system in action.

Ancient Egypt placed a high value on justice. So captured thieves would first have to pay back four times the amount they stole, but then they would also spend time in prison.[2] If someone physically hurt a person, the offender would first be physically beaten in front of the entire community before then being brought to jail for a substantial season of time. The Egyptian judicial system was groundbreaking for its time.

What I found fascinating about this system was the Egyptians' focus on educating their criminals. They did not view prison solely as punishment but more as a repro-gramming. Prisoners were not looked at as problems but as students who needed teaching. "Ancient Egypt created the great human value of educating criminals through keeping them in jail, to apply justice's principal and benefit society. . . . Jails . . . worked on rehabilitation to convert criminals to ethical persons that benefit and can adapt with the Egyptian society."[3]

Educators would make their regular rounds to edu-cated prisoners in the prison system of ancient Egypt. A prisoner would walk into the cell a nuisance but walk out a prized citizen. There was no community college or adult education in the Egyptian system, so the only adults who got any extra education were prisoners. This was the system that Joseph entered. Many times when we think of prisoners in ancient Egypt, we picture slaves building pyramids, but that was not Joseph's situation. He was put in the same prison "where the king's prisoners were con-fined" (Gen. 39:20).

Could the education system be the ultimate reason that Joseph was thrown into prison? Joseph was raised hundreds of miles away from Egypt. He would have been unfamiliar with the customs, the language, the traditions, and the overall culture. So while Joseph thought he was simply going to the slammer, he was actually going to school.

The season might not have made sense for Joseph, but it was certainly significant for him. Looking at Joseph's story now, we can see how God is always sovereign and works all things together for good. Joseph took advantage of the opportunity to learn in the prison what he would need in the palace. It is not clear if Joseph knew this education was going to be beneficial for his future, but the overall takeaway is that he didn't spend his prison season weeping; he spent it working.

God wants to teach you something during your dark days too. The opportunists ask themselves, "What can I learn during this dark season?" We all want the mountain moments, but the most defining and developing moments are usually found in the valley. Joseph would spend the next decade in a prison where he would get his honorary degree in Egyptian culture. Little did he realize how crucial this would be in the next season of his life. It was unfair that Joseph was imprisoned, but those life-changing lessons were the advantage.

REBOUNDING THROUGH RELATIONSHIPS

The irony of the loneliness of prison is that we can't win alone. The next part of the story reveals that Joseph leaned into two key relationships in his dark season. Genesis 39:21 says, "The LORD was with him; he showed him kindness and granted him favor in the eyes of the prison warden." Joseph thrived in prison because of his relationship with God and his relationship with his leadership.

God builds his kingdom through relationships. For instance, key relationships will be the deciding factor between doors that either open or close. Good relationships will always take work, and healthy ones will never happen accidentally. They are always built intentionally.

I like to say relationships that work take work. If only everyone could learn this truth early on in life. If you want the relationship to work, you have to work on it. Marriages will fail if there is no effort. Friendships fizzle if people stop caring. Families are a mess if attention isn't given to them. Organizations won't succeed if the teamwork is overlooked. It's clear that any type of relationship will work only if the work is put in.

Our Christian faith is defined by relationship, not by religion. If you have believed rules and restrictions should be emphasized, you couldn't be further from the truth. Jesus came to reestablish a relationship between man and God. You were created for and you thrive the most when you are in relationship with God.

Jesus modeled for us a life of unhindered relationship with God the Father as well as healthy relationships with people. His example shows that even during the best and worst days, relationships are worth investing in. Honestly, this is so much easier in theory than in reality, so let's examine how Jesus thrived in relationship with God and with people. First, in the chaos of ministry, Scripture tells us that "Jesus often withdrew to lonely places and prayed" (Luke 5:16). He leaned into a rhythm of spending time with God because he knew how primarily crucial that relationship was.

Jesus employed a three-part strategy to intentionally build a close relationship with God the Father. He set a time, he had a specific place, and he had an intentional plan. Let me break this down because I think it will help your relationship with God and your relationships with people.

Jesus had a specific *time* for prayer. This was something seen in his life, and it is also necessary for each of us who wants to grow and invest in what we've been given. If you don't manage your time, someone else will. Jesus was a master of making his time work for him. We see in Mark 1:35 that Jesus made good use of the predawn hours: "Very early in the morning, while it was still dark, Jesus got up, left the house and went off to a solitary place, where he prayed." Days that end wrong usually start wrong. Jesus understood the importance of starting his day in prayer. Mornings may be impossible for you. I get it. So here is my challenge for you: find a time in your day that you can be intentional with, and then make an appointment with God and keep it. Put that quality time on your calendar and be consistent every day. Our greatest goals are not made in a day. They are made through daily commitment.

Jesus also had a specific *place* where he prayed. Luke 22:39 tells us that "He came out and went, as was His habit, to the Mount of Olives; and the disciples also followed Him"

(NASB). Luke reported this as if it was common knowledge to the disciples. Jesus had the habit of going to a special place for time with God. In my own life, I have found this to be a game changer. I have a spot in my house that is marked as holy, set apart for time with the Lord. It is the place where I can remove all distractions and focus on my relationship with God. So find your own prayer spot, and be sure to remove all distractions so you can truly focus on your relationship with God.

Jesus also had a specific *plan* when he got alone with God the Father. His prayer life wasn't random, it was always strategic. When his disciples observed him, they were so blown away by the intensity and intimacy of his prayer life that they asked him, "Lord, teach us to pray" (Luke 11:1). It was out of this conversation that Jesus revealed what we now call the Lord's Prayer. Let's walk through Matthew 6:9–13 (NASB) together.

> **"Our Father who is in heaven"**–Connect with God relationally.
>
> **"Hallowed be Your name"**–Worship his name.
>
> **"Your kingdom come. Your will be done, on earth as it is in heaven"**–Pray his agenda will be first.
>
> **"Give us this day our daily bread"**–Depend on him for everything.
>
> **"And forgive us our debts, as we also have forgiven our debtors"**–Get our hearts right with God and with people.
>
> **"And do not lead us into temptation, but deliver us from evil"**–Engage in spiritual warfare.

"For Yours is the kingdom and the power and the glory forever"–Express faith in God's ability.

This plan of Jesus was structured beautifully around an intentional purpose. And this is just one of many plans seen throughout Scripture of how to engage in a deeper level with God. Personally, I like to change up my prayer structure a few times a year so it never becomes routine and mindless. We must always keep in mind the heart of prayer is relationship, and your relationship with God will sustain you when everything else in life fails you. He is "a friend who sticks closer than a brother" (Prov. 18:24). This is an amazing gift that is one of the privileges our prayer life enhances.

Now, back to where we left Joseph in prison. Like Jesus, he was also very relationally minded. He first leaned into his relationship with God before investing in any other relationship. This is the blueprint for each of us. You will have greater joy and growth in your relationships when God is given first place in your priorities. I am a better friend, a better coworker, a better boss, a better parent, and a better spouse when I am connected with God.

In his darkest moments, Joseph leaned into his relationship with God. It is this message James gave when he wrote, "Come near to God and he will come near to you" (4:8). Maybe you are in a dark time right now too. Let this be a gentle reminder. Reach out to God. If you have distanced yourself, then return to the Father, who holds his arms wide open. Bring him your sin, your baggage, and your disappointments. God gives a fresh start. He walks with us in

With God first in our lives, we win.

the darkness, and he is the light that helps us overcome. No matter the situation, with God first in our lives, we win.

Jesus also modeled for us the importance of winning at relationships with people. During his three years of public ministry, he invested a significant amount of his time in twelve ordinary, unschooled men. The crowds of people were never neglected, but the Twelve received his full attention. He understood that gathering a multitude of thousands was less significant than making legitimate disciples. If Jesus believed in the necessity of investing oneself in others, then we should believe it too.

Our social media age gives a modern-day analogy of this example that Jesus lived out. The present-day crowds of people in our lives often exist behind a screen, and while they have needs Christ can minister to, our biggest investment should be those flesh and blood people closest to us. Unfortunately, to the detriment of those around us, so much of our attention is often focused on winning the crowd. This is why, when it comes to relationships, it is important to keep our motives pure and our focus steady. The measure of true success is whether those who know me the best are the ones who respect me the most. And we can trust that our time with just a few will never be wasted. Just think, it is from Jesus' intentional investment into a few that the gospel went around the globe. He made the most of every opportunity in his season here on earth.

Joseph did the same during his dark seasons. He couldn't win with the masses, but he did win with the men directly in front of him. He found opportunity even during oppression. This is an unfair advantage you can embrace. Winning with the right people will always be beneficial.

I think it is notable that Joseph found favor with the prison warden. (More about that a bit later.)

It is true that Joseph experienced a lot of tragedy, but his experience shows that with the right people, circumstances can become more positive. This is because a lot of times, the quality of your relationships determines the quantity of your joy. So, to maximize our joy, we each must learn to win at the relationships that matter most. I have found three building blocks in every healthy relationship: respect, listening, and time.

Everyone deserves some level of *respect*. Personally, I do not want to be around people who merely tolerate me. It is much more encouraging to surround myself with people who celebrate me. The same is true the other way. I want to be someone who celebrates the people around me. The disciple Peter wrote, "Show proper respect to everyone, love the family of believers, fear God, honor the emperor" (1 Peter 2:17). This ruler Peter was referring to was Nero, a harsh persecutor of Christians. The implication from this scripture is that even Nero deserved some respect. So we honor people, not because it's easy but because we are honorable.

Another building block for relationships is *listening*. You might agree that we have a massive listening problem in our world today. Edgar Watson Howe said, "No man would listen to you talk if he didn't know it was his turn next."[4] How true. This could be one of the greatest breakdowns in our relationships. We talk too much and listen too little. God gave us two ears and one mouth. We should listen twice as much as we speak.

In James we read, "My dear brothers and sisters, take note of this: Everyone should be quick to listen, slow to speak and slow to become angry" (1:19). This is wisdom for the ages. If you want healthy relationships, you must make sure you are listening. People do not care what you know until they know that you care. If you want to win with others, start by listening to them. That doesn't mean you have to do everything they say, but it does mean when they are speaking you are actively engaged in hearing them. People are most honored when they feel like they are being heard. Dale Carnegie said, "You can make more friends in two weeks by becoming a good listener than you can in two years trying to get other people to listen to you."[5] You will win, just by listening.

The last crucial ingredient for relationships is *time*. Time is much like having $1,440 deposited in your bank account daily. However, you cannot save it up for a rainy day or retirement because at the end of the day, you lose the balance of what you did not spend. You are given 1,440 minutes every day to spend however you like, but at the end of the day, your time is gone and will never be available again. If you do not use it, you lose it.

The way we invest in relationships is by giving people our most valuable asset, our time.

Katie and I both find ourselves getting so busy that it is hard to find time to invest in our marriage. We have tried to fix this problem with a system we applied early on called the Seven, Seven, Seven Rule. Every seven days we try to get some form of a date in. This is hard with five kids, and it often doesn't involve candles or fancy dinners, but it is always worth it. Every date, we try to put our phones away and focus on each other. Around every seven weeks, we try to do a day away or a night away. We have come to love these little mini trips that help us cultivate intimacy and conversation. Every seven months we do some sort of vacation. I love my kids, but a true relaxing vacation isn't with the whole family, it is just me and my spouse. Katie and I work hard at saving money just to take wild and crazy getaways. We have been able to travel the world together, and other times we have just gone an hour or two away and stayed in a hotel. To foster quality time in marriage, you don't have to follow our system, but find something that works for you and be consistent.

Let me just speak into one more area of your relationships. Joseph was intentional about the prison warden, the person in charge of the prison. This showed Joseph's strategic mindset. Everyone is important, but not everyone has the ability to open doors for you. Who is that person who holds the key for your future? Win with him or her. When I became a youth pastor, I didn't have to win with all the staff, but I did want to win with my boss. I was intentional about showing respect, about listening, and about giving him my undivided time. Because of that investment, so many doors have opened for me.

For Joseph's story, "the warden paid no attention to anything under Joseph's care" (Gen. 39:23). This is the goal in your relationship with your boss. When you invest in making that relationship healthy, eventually your boss will trust you and not micromanage you. This was how my relationship was with the pastor I worked under for six years. Even though I don't work for him any longer, he is a great mentor and friend. Never burn a bridge you might have to walk over again one day. Fight for healthy relationships.

THE UNFAIR ADVANTAGE: WORKING WHILE YOU ARE WAITING

An example of Joseph's mindfulness toward others occurred when, even in the darkness, he noticed concerns and he reached out to help. Imprisoned with him were two of Pharaoh's officials, the chief cupbearer and the chief baker. Joseph saw they were upset, and he asked, "Why do you look so sad today?" (Gen. 40:7). They explained they both had vivid dreams and didn't know what they meant. Remember where Joseph's dream landed him in the beginning of our story? It would have been so easy for him to say, "Dreams can't be trusted. Ignore them and run away!" But Joseph recognized God was at work in these dreams, and refusing to be a pessimist, he looked for how he could help. Like Joseph, we as followers of Jesus should not be stuck in the despair of our circumstances. Instead, we should find opportunities to see where God is working and how we can work alongside him. Don't let the failures of one season keep you from taking faith steps in this season. Joseph allowed God to use him in the prison cell. He seized the opportunity. This is an unfair advantage. There is unique opportunity to work while we wait.

Joseph had dreamed before. Interestingly, though, nowhere in Scripture, until this point, do we see that Joseph had any kind of gift for interpreting dreams. Only in the darkness of prison, over many years, Joseph matured into the man who could now be used in the way God had intended. You never know how the time in the dark will strengthen and equip you for what God is calling you to next.

In 2004, I flew across the country to do an internship at a small church outside of Portland, Oregon. The church had a huge heart for global missions, and since my dream was to live and work in Asia, I was excited about getting my feet into the work of overseas ministry.

As soon as I arrived, the pastor, Werner, sat me down and gave me the game plan for the twelve weeks I would be part of their team. When he told me that the first month would be spent in children's ministry, I quickly interrupted him. Thanks but no thanks! I told him I appreciated the opportunity, but I did not need to know anything about children's ministry. I was sure I would never work with children. My goal was to preach the gospel and to see it taken into the four corners of the world. I respectfully asked him to let me focus on what I was passionate about.

As convincing as I thought I was, Werner declined my proposition. For one whole month, my job would be children's ministry and vacation Bible school. My fate had been sealed and I was frustrated!

The first few days were a struggle, and I spent most of my time counting down the moments until I could transition to "real ministry" with "real humans." Thankfully, I finally crucified my flesh and decided to become fully present.

The theme of our VBS was a tropical volcanic island. We spent sixty-plus hours a week strategizing how to give these Pacific Northwest kids a tropical experience. Game day approached and we had three hundred kids present. The event finished with my favorite part, a ten-foot-tall handmade volcano erupting. Like the volcano, the entire event was chaos, but a major win for everyone.

I ended up making the most of my monthlong children's ministry stint, but still finished believing the time had been pointless. Years later, though, my first job in ministry was to oversee the outreaches and programs for five thousand kids on the tropical island of Sri Lanka. Part of my job was a VBS-type ministry every day for six months. And while I should have been clueless on how to do this, thanks to my time in that small Portland church, I had an abundance of resources to pull from. Now, I'm not comparing my time with children to Joseph's time in prison. But I am saying that no season is wasted, even the ones we want to move on from. God can use the most mundane moments, as well as the darkest days, when we are faithful.

It is easy to want to focus only on investing in our strengths, but at times God likes to develop some of our weaknesses as well. You do not know what the future holds, but God does. So if you feel you are in a place where your strengths aren't thriving, don't get discouraged. It could be that God is working on a weakness to use down the road.

I do CrossFit. I hate that we are this far into the book without me admitting this, because the first rule of CrossFit is making sure you tell everyone that you do CrossFit. A few years back I took this hobby to the next level by enrolling in my first team competition. I had been preparing, and it was at my happy place, the beach, so I thought it would be easy. It wasn't. My team got destroyed. In the middle of our struggling, I realized the problem. The competition was full of exercises that I was weak in. It was all those workouts I had been avoiding in the gym. What I know now about CrossFit, which applies to life as well, is that to succeed we need to strengthen our entire body, not just the places where we are already strong.

People are not as strong as their greatest strength; they are as weak as their greatest weakness. Work on your weaknesses. If God has you in a season where you feel stretched in something you aren't great at, embrace it. He knows what's ahead of you that you will need to be prepared for.

In 2017, I took a plunge and started pursuing my doctorate. It took three busy, intense years, but I finally completed it during the 2020 global pandemic. Honestly, there were multiple classes I absolutely hated. They required five to ten pages a week in doctoral-level writing. This was painful for me. I thought it was pointless and a waste of time.

Over those three years my weakness in writing was strengthened. The skills I learned during such a busy season of endless papers prepared me later when I knew God was calling me to write this book.

With God, nothing is by accident. It is encouraging to know that if he has you working on it, he is going to work through it. What is that weakness God has you working on right now? What is that skill God could be trying to strengthen in your life? Don't waste this season.

Joseph ended up accurately interpreting the dreams of

the chief cupbearer and chief baker. He made the most of this opportunity in prison, and he had high hopes it would help him too. I have to warn you, though, the investments you make might not immediately pay off. Joseph asked the cupbearer, "When all goes well with you, remember me and show me kindness; mention me to Pharaoh and get me out of this prison. I was forcibly carried off from the land of the Hebrews, and even here I have done nothing to deserve being put in a dungeon" (Gen. 40:14–15). He was frustrated, and he believed this relationship would help set him free. Unfortunately, he was wrong. Instead of finding freedom, Joseph was left alone and forgotten.

DISCUSSION QUESTIONS

During this chapter we discovered that opportunities are available during seasons of oppression. It is important to learn to identify the work that needs to be done during your dark seasons. These three discussion questions should help facilitate that discussion.

1. Looking back, when have you seized an opportunity or made the most of a relationship during a difficult season?
2. What opportunity is available for you to take advantage of during this season?
3. What relationship do you need to lean into? How can you develop that relationship?

THE FORGOTTEN FAITHFUL

*The chief cupbearer, however, did not
remember Joseph; he forgot him.*
GENESIS 40:23

When two full years had passed . . .
GENESIS 41:1

It's probably safe to say that most of us have felt forgotten at some time in our lives. It may be easy for you to recall a particularly painful moment of neglect. It's a very hurtful and lonely state to feel like no one remembers you, like no one cares. This is why it is especially moving to hear that

Joseph was, by all appearances, forgotten by everyone for a decade—ten years of sitting in a prison for a crime he did not commit. It would seem that he was even forgotten by God. Where was God during that decade? We have all had these moments where the dream comes from God, and then he seems to disappear and we wonder if God has given up on us and the entire process.

There seems to be a bit of breakthrough when Joseph interprets the cupbearer's dream. Joseph, longing to get out of prison, had pleaded with the cupbearer to remember him. You can almost imagine the hope in Joseph's eyes when he sees his freedom in this man whom he had helped. He was so close. And then, like the prison door slamming shut, Genesis 40:23 says, "The chief cupbearer, however, did not remember Joseph; he forgot him." Ugh! After enduring years of wrongful prison time, his one shot for justice had disappeared. So, the days turned into another two seemingly hopeless years.

You have to wonder, during all this time as a slave and then a prisoner, what was going through Joseph's mind? *Where is God? What happened to that dream? Was it all in my head? Where is the father who said he loved me so much? Did my brothers finally regret their decision and are they looking for me? Has Potiphar learned about his wife's lie that put me in prison? Will he come to the prison soon to make things right?* The last hopeful thought may have been, *The cupbearer should be coming any day now. He told me he would help.* But no one ever came for Joseph. People failed him time and again. And so, he was left, alone and forgotten, for years and years.

What was your forgotten moment? Maybe your parents forgot to pick you up from school. Or your friends forgot to invite you to a party. Your boss may have forgotten about the promotion. Or your heart may be broken by your spouse's forgetting their vow. Being forgotten is like a kick in the gut. It can come in many ways, but it's always painful.

David, who would one day go down in history as the famous giant killer and king of Israel, also knew the pain of being forgotten. When the prophet Samuel showed up at his home to anoint the future king, David's father brought out his seven older sons and intentionally excluded David. He left him in the field tending the sheep. He was sure there was no way David would be the son God would choose.

As Samuel looked at the eldest brother, he was at first inclined to agree with the dad that this was the look of a true king. But God stopped Samuel by saying such a relevant word for each of us. "Do not consider his appearance or his height, for I have rejected him. The LORD does not look at the things people look at. People look at the outward appearance, but the LORD looks at the heart" (1 Sam. 16:7). It would have been common to look for the man who was the strongest, the tallest, and the most handsome, but God was looking for something else—something that could only be found within.

David's dad may have forgotten about him, but God didn't. After his father called for David to come home, the Bible tells us, "Samuel took the horn of oil and anointed him in the presence of his brothers, and from that day on the Spirit of the LORD came powerfully upon David" (1 Sam. 16:13).

FORGOTTEN BY MAN, FORGED BY GOD

The point I am making with the story of David is that people may forget you, but God never has. You may be forgotten by man, but you are never forgotten by God. And in the pain, he is working. Those moments when you feel forgotten are the moments when God is forging you, building you into something new.

When we think of diamonds, it is easy to picture how bright, eye-catching, and obvious they are. When a woman first gets engaged, it seems like every girl within a mile radius immediately notices the diamond ring. What a lot of us don't think of, though, is the beginning stages of the diamond, the season when it is unnoticed and forgotten. Diamonds are made one hundred miles deep in the earth, in areas known as the mantle. The temperatures reach a sweltering 2,200 degrees Fahrenheit. If the lava-like temperature wasn't intense enough, the pressure in the area is enormous, exceeding 725,000 pounds per square inch.[1] This astronomical heat and pressure combine to antagonize the unnoticed, overlooked lumps of coal in the earth, and given enough time they are transformed into very valuable diamonds.

How long does it take to create a diamond? If you are thinking just a few days of discomfort, you would be wrong. It's actually not days, months, decades, or centuries. Scientists believe this: "At least hundreds of millions of years old, but in most cases billions of years old, anywhere from one to three billion years old, a time when the earth was probably hotter than it is today and so conditions were perhaps more appropriate for diamond growth."[2] I hope that helps with perspective. Nothing great happens overnight. Things take time. Coal is common, unimpressive, and cheap. It's what Santa gives the naughty kids at Christmas. It is definitely not what you propose with. As undesirable as it is, it's hard to believe coal is a potential diamond that never developed. In their finished state, diamonds are some of the most sought-after treasures. They are dreamed about, cherished, and passed on generation to generation. So it's remarkable that the most valuable diamonds are simply coal that endured the forgotten stage. During the time that no one sees the diamond, it is being made into something beautiful.

You may be hidden from people but not from God. The pressure is for a purpose. The heat can make you healthy. Embrace the process of allowing the Lord to work in a season where no one sees you. God is creating a diamond. Don't sell yourself short, and don't get out of the process early. I know it's tempting, but something beautiful is being formed.

IT ALWAYS TAKES LONGER

How do we trust that God has not forgotten us? The key is to remember that God's timing is not our timing. It always feels like it takes longer with God. His timing is not our timing, but it's the right time. A common theme for the heroes of faith throughout Scripture is the time they spent waiting on the promise from God. For example, it took years for Noah to build the ark, for Moses to get to the promised land, and for the Lord Jesus to complete his ministry on earth. This shows God is very interested in the process that takes us to the product. The journey is just as important as the destination. I am going to let you in on a little secret: things will usually take longer than you want them to take.

One of my daily goals in life is beating the time on Google Maps. I am whatever personality type has the obsession to beat the GPS no matter where I may be going. If it says I will arrive at 6:55 p.m., my goal is to get that number into the 6:40s. It is a skill I have spent my life refining.

When I travel alone, I am almost always able to beat my goal. However, when my family is in the car, it is impossible. Family road trips always take longer than I want them to. I have five kids under ten years old, and every Christmas we travel to my in-laws' place in North Georgia. The GPS tells us it takes nine hours, but it sadly always takes us ten-plus. Why? Because I am traveling with something greater than just me.

You might feel alone, but let me assure you, your life is bigger than you are. We live in an age of instant gratification, but there is no overnight success when it comes to legacy. It will take you longer than you want it to take, but it will be greater than you can imagine. The rule is universal; if I am traveling with more people or more cargo, it will take longer. As the African proverb puts it, "If you want to go fast, go alone. If you want to go far, go together."

When stuck in a slow-moving season, where things are taking longer than we want, I have found there are usually two possible reasons. It could be *disobedience*, or it could be *development*. Let's start with disobedience because this one is the hardest to hear. Some setbacks are undeniably out of our control, but other times we are completely to blame. To move forward, we need to recognize that and take ownership.

Until we assume responsibility for our mess, we will never get out of our situation. The children of Israel are a great example. According to Google Maps, a person should be able to walk from Egypt to Jerusalem in roughly 190 hours. Experts believe if Moses and the children of Israel had taken a straight shot to Jerusalem, it would have taken twenty-five to forty days. Again, if you want to go fast, go alone, but if you want to go far, go together. A big group slows it down quite a bit.

If you remember the story, it didn't take forty days; it took forty *years*. They repeatedly disobeyed God, hardening their hearts toward him, and the consequence was this: "Your children will be shepherds here for forty years, suffering for your unfaithfulness, until the last of your bodies lies in the wilderness" (Num. 14:33). That hurts. Disobedience creates long delays so God can do some much-needed work in our hearts.

If something is taking longer than I want, my first step is going to be checking my heart. Do I have an obedience issue? Is there something God told me to do that I have not done? Maybe there is something I was supposed to give up that I have been holding on to. Deuteronomy 30:15–16 says, "See, I set before you today life and prosperity, death and destruction. For I command you today to love the LORD your God, to walk in obedience to him, and to keep his commands, decrees and laws; then you will live and increase, and the LORD your God will bless you in the land you are entering to possess."

We can't live life stubbornly choosing our own path while expecting to also end up in God's plan. Giving your life to Jesus makes him both your Lord and Savior. Most people have agreed to the Savior part, but the Lord part is a little tougher. It's difficult to relinquish control. C. S. Lewis emphasized the crucial choice that determines every person's eventual fate when he said, "There are only two kinds of people in the end: those who say to God, 'Thy will be done,' and those to whom God says, in the end, '*Thy* will be done.'"[3]

Disobedience is not always the reason for a delay in life. Sometimes it is simply because of development that still needs to happen. Many of our problems are not punishments for bad behavior, but rather they are preparation from God for something else. The children of Israel were in the desert for far too long, and one reason was they needed the time it would take to learn lessons they would need later in life. For instance, God sent miracle bread, manna, for them to eat every day. Deuteronomy 8:3 says, "He humbled you, causing you to hunger and then feeding you with manna, which neither you nor your ancestors had known, to teach you that man does not live on bread alone but on every word that comes from the mouth of the LORD." They had a lesson to learn that was bigger than just their hunger being met. God is our provider. And we are to rely on him for every need. These are lessons you only learn in the wilderness.

We stay in the wilderness until we learn everything we

are supposed to. We shouldn't interpret the seasons as if God were angry with us. Rather, we are to look at them as a tool he is using to develop us. Preparation is necessary for the promised land he has in mind, even if it looks like forty years in a wilderness, ten years in a prison, or four weeks in a children's ministry internship.

To trust God is to trust in his timing. When describing the birth of Jesus, Scripture tells us, "When the right time came, God sent his Son" (Gal. 4:4 NLT). God is strategic in his timing. He knew when the perfect time would be for his Son to come on the scene. It is the same for you. The right time and environment have been planned out. It might take longer than you thought, but with God at the wheel, it will be better than you thought.

> Preparation is necessary for the promised land he has in mind.

My wife, Katie, and I got married in 2010. The time has flown by. She is truly the love of my life and no one gets me quite like her. But our story wasn't always a fairy tale. After lots of back-and-forth feelings throughout our college years, we finally got together and dated the last six months of my final year. After graduating, I immediately went overseas as a missionary to Sri Lanka. We said the sad farewells but promised to stay committed in our long-distance relationship. Thanks to calls, cards, and emails, we spent the next six months bonding through lots of talking. Over time, Katie became more and more invested in us, while I became more and more invested in my job. That Christmas I came home and, taking her by complete surprise, I broke up with her. She was devastated. I was selfish. She thought we would be getting married. I just wanted to change the world. She was in love. I was in love . . . with the idea of being single.

For the next four years, we barely spoke. (Yes, *years*.) Because we had lots of mutual friends, we saw each other occasionally, but living far apart, we both moved on with our lives. Katie will tell you that at first she was devastated by our breakup, but she ended up embracing the season of singleness. She graduated from college and spent time in Ethiopia volunteering in a Mother Teresa home. While there she received a renewed vision of what God was calling her to do next.

Her trip to Africa highlighted her heart to help people who are hurting, so she enrolled in nursing school and graduated with her RN degree a few years later. She had been forgotten, abandoned by the man she loved. But God never left her. He used this dark, hidden season in her life to develop her into the compassionate and skilled world changer she is today. Years later, I had grown up a lot, and in a season of prayer and fasting, God placed Katie on my heart. It was supernatural and clear that this was the right time and she was the right girl. I drove down to where she lived, seven hours away, and told her that she was going to be my wife. Unfortunately, she said, "No way!" So I asked her to take a month and pray about it.

In that time God spoke to her in a similar way, and one month later we were dating. Two months later we were engaged, and we have now experienced over a decade of a happy, healthy marriage with the arrival of five amazing kids along the way. The original dream of those two young college students finally became a reality. It just took longer than either of us expected. Why? Probably because of a lot of disobedience on my part, but also some development was necessary for both of us. It might have taken longer than we hoped, but it has been way better than we expected. That is the fruit of trusting God's timing.

Joseph found himself in his own wilderness predicament. He was a forgotten dreamer who was rejected by his brothers, a forgotten employee underpaid and undervalued by his new boss, and a forgotten victim wrongfully accused by his boss's wife. Each step in this wilderness led to the prison where he had been trapped for years. It was probably the darkest season of his life. Maybe he thought his life was over. But God had a plan.

PLANTED, NOT BURIED

My wife got into gardening—once. Thanks to Pinterest, we invested a few hundred dollars into something she assured me would end up paying for itself.

The problem is that plants come to my house to die. And that is exactly what happened to this garden. My wife started by excitedly buying the pots and seeds, planting everything carefully, and setting it all out in the backyard. It was off to a great start. But then she forgot all about them. I don't think she ever checked on anything again after that first day! About a year or so later, we ended up moving, and when I went to the hidden parts of our backyard to make sure everything was cleared out, lo and behold, there were all the neglected pots with dead plants barely making it out of the dirt. The biggest surprise, though, was that, even as forgotten as it was, one of the containers had ended up growing this enormous cabbage plant. It had been sitting by our air conditioning unit, so I have a theory that some kind of AC fluids must have mutated it into the massive size it turned out to be. But whatever the cause, that hidden seed obviously had more potential than we ever realized!

Even the best gardeners understand that seeds are pointless unless they are planted. When they get planted, though, they have the power of multiplication. Similarly, we are like seeds that, when planted in the right conditions, can grow into something beautiful.

Planting and burying look very similar. In both cases, the ground is opened, something is put inside, and dirt is spread until it completely disappears. But although the action is the same, the definitions of planting and burying are very different. When something is buried, the best part of it is gone and its future is over. When something is planted, however, it stays hidden for a season but then produces a harvest much better than before.

This distinction can be helpful for us when we go into a dark season. That forgotten place, that dark hole, is not where you are buried. Rather, perhaps you are being planted. You can trust the Master Gardener will produce something significant from this season. Jesus reassured us, "My Father is the gardener" (John 15:1). He did not tell us, "My Father is the undertaker." He didn't bring you to this spot to bury you, but to begin a great work within you.

Looking back on my life, I thank God he didn't give me everything I prayed for. There were seasons early on that I craved more opportunities and a wider influence. But I realize now there is no way I could have handled it. It would have been like a firework that flew high quickly, made a big explosion, and then fizzled out because there was no substance.

Be careful what you pray for. Stop asking God to deliver you from the very thing he is using to develop you. The seed could get frustrated because it is not seen or it is not moving at a faster pace. But it would be a mistake for the seed to get delivered from the soil before its time. Often we are praying that God would deliver us from the job, the relationship, the employer, the struggle, the hardship, and we don't realize these things are the soil in which we grow the most.

So in the planting season, when you are thick in the soil, let your roots grow down deep. We discussed this a little in the section on integrity. The larger the tree, the greater the roots. If you want God to do something big, start by letting him do something deep. Some of the largest and oldest trees in the world are the sequoias, which rise to over three hundred feet tall and end up weighing nearly two million pounds. These massive trees have managed to stay upright for over three thousand years because of their incredible root systems. "A mature sequoia's roots can occupy over 1 acre of earth and contain over 90,000 cubic feet of soil."[4] Their widespread and large roots keep these trees living for centuries. Paul challenged us, "Let your roots grow down into him, and let your lives be built on him" (Col. 2:7 NLT).

Always be growing, "rooted and built up in him" (Col. 2:7). Our aim as Christ followers is to continually grow deep in our relationship with Christ. Paul gave us this challenge when he wrote, "I want to know Christ" (Phil. 3:10). This is a deep pursuit after God. This is not religion; "know" here is the same word used for a spouse knowing another spouse. It is a lifelong pursuit. Your life should be marked by growing. When you stop growing you start dying. I want to live in such a way that I keep growing up, growing deep, and growing wide until the day I die. Let's be planted, not buried.

THE POWER OF PERSISTENCE

"Fool me once, shame on you. Fool me twice, shame on me." This saying is used to encourage people not to fall for the same gimmick twice. Joseph didn't live with this type of attitude. He experienced incident after incident of betrayal. His eleven brothers, his master Potiphar, Potiphar's wife, and the cupbearer had all turned their backs on him in one way or another. If Joseph were like most of us, he would spend the rest of his life talking about how terrible people are and how deeply he was mistreated. He would have thickened his skin, refusing to interact with another person who might fail him once again. Joseph was different, though. He knew the power of persistence.

My senior year of high school, a buddy and I entered an outdoor racquetball tournament at the local community college. We were young, had played racquetball for years, and knew that our competition was substantially older than we were. So we walked into the competition with all the cockiness of the overzealous teenagers we were. That day left us flat on our backs, absolutely destroyed by each one of our opponents. Out of the dozens of people who showed up to play, my friend and I came in dead last.

It was a two-day tournament, so we prepared ourselves for another day of absolute failure. When we woke up the next morning, though, torrential storms had taken over the entire city. I checked the radar and it looked like everything would clear soon, so my friend and I scrambled through the storm to our cars and made it to the courts a few minutes early. When we arrived, we discovered something interesting: we were the only ones who had braved the rain and shown up. The tournament managers waited a while before finally just agreeing to let my buddy and I play against each other for first and second place. I am proud to say that in the Pensacola racquetball competition of 2002, I finished in the top two places on the leaderboard. Which place is up to your imagination. We won simply by showing up—by persisting.

David showed up to fight Goliath in full faith. Goliath was a force to be reckoned with. The Israelites viewed him as unbeatable. But David didn't cower. The Bible tells us that before walking onto the battlefield, he chose five stones to attack the giant with. Why five stones? It could be because he didn't think he could hit him on the first one. In grabbing five stones, he made the decision that if he missed, he would not quit and run away. He would keep throwing until the last stone was gone.

This is the attitude it takes to win. If I don't bring the

giant down with the first stone, I will keep going. Keep fighting. Failure is an event, not a person, so don't ever call yourself one. If you have tried and it did not work, get back up. Falling down is an accident. Staying down is a choice.

Proverbs 24:16 says, "Though the righteous fall seven times, they rise again." Don't give up on whatever it is that you feel called to. Keep trying. If you can't trust yourself to keep going, get around some people who will encourage you on. Accountability partners, small groups, and counseling are all great sources. Pray for the right people to surround you in your battle as you keep showing up.

Stop making excuses and start making attempts. After coming in close to last after my first CrossFit competition, I felt like quitting. But I let the frustration of losing drive me to train harder. I still have never come close to winning a competition, but I am stronger than I would have been otherwise and so I am going to keep going. What have you failed at? It is unfair that it didn't work the first time. I get that. But keep going. You aren't responsible for the victory, but you are responsible for the participation.

Long after Joseph was left forgotten in prison, Pharaoh had a dream no one could interpret. Suddenly, the cup-bearer remembered the man who had interpreted a dream for him. He ran and told Pharaoh what had happened those two years earlier. And finally, Pharaoh called for Joseph to come before him. When Joseph arrived, Pharaoh said, "I had a dream, and no one can interpret it. But I have heard it said of you that when you hear a dream you can interpret it" (Gen. 41:15).

"I cannot do it." This is the phrase that Joseph used in

response to Pharaoh. This is the normal response we give when we are presented a challenge that we have tried before and failed at. Joseph had interpreted dreams in the past, and it left him stuck in prison. But Joseph also understood the power of persistence. His response didn't end there. He said, "I cannot do it . . . but God will give Pharaoh the answer he desires" (Gen. 41:16). Joseph was back! He was ready to rely on God's power to give him the strength to try again. We all need this fresh reliance on God's power to show up as we try again after failing. We need God with every shaking step as we refuse to give up, continually praying, "God help me persevere."

THE UNFAIR ADVANTAGE: NOT QUITTING

In 2005, before Apple became the massive empire it is today, I bought $1,000 of its stock right before I moved overseas to Sri Lanka. Being so focused on my new life in a new country, I forgot about the stock until I arrived back in the States for Christmas. I was reminded of it when a friend called to let me know that the stock had *doubled*. I was shocked. I had made $1,000 without doing anything.

So of course . . . I sold it. It hurts me to write that. I cashed out early. I decided to use my unexpected earnings for a great Christmas. By conservative estimates, if I had left the stock untouched, today it would be worth 130 times what I invested in 2005—somewhere around $130,000! This makes my heart sick.

Quitting at something is almost like cashing out early.

It can be tempting to want to move on to greener pastures, but we should never sacrifice the calling on our lives for instant gratification. So we wait and we trust in God. Whatever it is you are praying for, you are closer today than you were yesterday. Every day in prison, Joseph had to wait and trust. When all seemed lost and no one remembered him, he remained faithful. And eventually the prison doors opened, and he was given the audience of a king.

While perseverance should be celebrated, let me be clear: there are some things you should quit. You should quit trying to please everyone. You should quit snacking so late at night. You should quit your endless scrolling on social media. You should quit going back to that toxic relationship. There are times when quitting is the healthy thing to do.

Along that line, there may be things you have wanted desperately to quit but for one reason or another have never succeeded. This can come in the form of addictions, compulsions, or attitudes that have felt impossible to shake. Try again. We cannot let past failures keep us from future successes. When Naaman came to Elisha to find healing from his leprosy, Elisha told him, "Go, wash yourself seven times in the Jordan, and your flesh will be restored, and you will be cleansed" (2 Kings 5:10). To Naaman, this advice seemed impractical. So he went away angry.

Many times, God uses the impractical to achieve the impossible. But before he got too far, Naaman reconsidered and decided to do what Elisha said. The Bible tells us, "He went down and dipped himself in the Jordan seven times, as the man of God had told him, and his flesh was restored and became clean like that of a young boy" (2 Kings 5:14). I bet this high-ranking official must have felt stupid after the second or third dunk into the water. But he kept dipping, and on the seventh dip, just as the prophet had said, his skin was cleansed.

Be encouraged about whatever you are struggling with. Keep trying. You never know when it will be your seventh dunk into the water and your miracle will happen. Research shows it takes between eight and thirty attempts for the average smoker to permanently quit smoking.[5] Keep going. Keep circling. Keep dunking. Your next attempt could very well be the one that works.

When you feel forgotten, stay faithful wherever you are, no matter the prison or the palace you find yourself in. Stay persistent and, whatever it is you are called to, don't give up. Many people love to dream, but few people actually see their dreams become reality. Why? Because obstacles, disappointments, and crises happen. But the key is not quitting when it gets tough. The people who have made it to their end goal are simply the ones who didn't quit when everyone else did, so keep pursuing the dream. Keep pursuing all that God has for you.

I started on the swim team at the age of six. I have always been tall and lanky, and my swim coaches would tell me I was made to be a good swimmer. There was only one problem: I hated going to practice. It was too early, too cold, and the clothing was way too little. So, not long after starting, I quit the team.

Michael Phelps was born eighteen months after me. He started the swim team when he was seven, a year older than the age I was when I started. He is one inch taller than me and my same weight. He was even diagnosed in sixth grade with attention deficit hyperactivity disorder (ADHD), just like I was. The major difference between the two of us, though, was that Michael never quit the swim team. By the age of ten, Phelps held the national record for his age group in the 100-meter butterfly.[6]

Despite similar body types and swimming histories, Michael Phelps would go on to win twenty-three Olympic gold medals, the most in human history. I, on the other hand, have won a total of zero gold medals and would never even have come close to qualifying to swim in a local competition. As newly signed-up swim team kids, Michael and I had many things in common. But the biggest difference between us is that he never quit.

If you have been holding on to a dream, don't give up. If you are tempted to let go, don't. If you are tempted to give in, don't. Your breakthrough might just be right around the corner. It is much easier to throw in the towel than it is to get back in the ring and keep fighting. But don't quit on the dream. History is made by those who didn't quit when it got tough.

History is made by those who didn't quit when it got tough.

How do we make this practical? By remembering what we are fighting for. We will always give in if we forget what the fight is all about. In marriage, Katie and I have had moments of being frustrated with each other, until one of us looks at the other and says, "What was this fight about again?" We laugh and realize we can't fight over something that's obviously not important enough to remember. While walking away from a fight is good for a healthy marriage, it's not good for a dream. If you feel like giving up, remember what it is that you're fighting for.

I know this is a little morbid, but sometimes I think about what I want said about me at my funeral. Imagining the people I love the most memorializing me in words is one of the best motivators to keep me going in those moments I want to quit. When I am fighting for the dream God has given me, I think about how I want to be remembered as someone who never stopped pursuing what God had called me to, even in the tough times. I like to think that every day of my life I am writing the script for my funeral. And even if I fail in accomplishments, I want to be remembered as someone who was always faithful—faithful to my call, faithful to my family, faithful to my church, and faithful to my God. It is an echo of Paul, who coincidentally wrote at the end of his life from a prison cell, "I have fought the good fight, I have finished the race, and I have remained faithful" (2 Tim. 4:7 NLT). Faithfulness transcends the success and notoriety the world craves. When we are faithful, we are never forgotten.

Joseph spent a decade forgotten in a prison cell, but through every dark day he remained faithful to the Lord. And those years of steadfast waiting were just what was needed when God brought him out of the prison and into the palace. The forgotten years were actually an unfair advantage that would help him later on. Are you in a forgotten season? Have you been waiting for something that hasn't come? It can be very difficult, and staying faithful is challenging. Maybe you feel like you've failed in your wait.

Maybe your doubts have taken over your dream. If so, be encouraged. Even when we are not faithful to our dream or our calling, God is still always faithful. I love the scripture from Mark 9:24: "I do believe; help me overcome my unbelief!" God can renew your faith, strengthen your resolve, and keep you from stumbling. As the psalmist declared, "Weeping may last for the night, but a shout of joy comes in the morning" (Ps. 30:5 NASB). Get ready and have faith. It's about to be morning.

DISCUSSION QUESTIONS

We all have moments when we feel forgotten, when life is being endured instead of enjoyed. We learned in this chapter to embrace these moments as defining instead of depressing. With God's help, we can learn something in the prison we might need in the palace. Let's talk a bit about how to keep going during difficult seasons.

1. What are you waiting for in this season of your life?
2. How are you leaning into your relationship with God during this waiting season?
3. What relationships can you invest in during this season?
4. What type of story do you want to eventually tell about your life?
5. What is the ultimate "why" that will motivate you when you are tempted to quit?

UNFAIR ADVANTAGE #7

THE LIMITED
LEADER

Then Pharaoh said to Joseph, "I am Pharaoh, but without your word no one will lift hand or foot in all Egypt." . . . Joseph was thirty years old when he entered the service of Pharaoh king of Egypt. And Joseph went out from Pharaoh's presence and traveled throughout Egypt. During the seven years of abundance the land produced plentifully. Joseph collected all the food produced in those seven years of abundance in Egypt and stored it in the cities. In each city he put the food grown in the fields surrounding it.

GENESIS 41:44, 46-48

Picture with me what it must have felt like for Joseph to walk out of that prison. His dirty, malnourished body may have ached with each step. His eyes, accustomed only to

157

darkness, may have had difficulty adjusting to their first view of sunlight in ten years. How surreal it must have felt to hear the prison doors shut behind him. For years he had been unjustly locked up and continually let down. But finally, he was free. And not only that, but he was trading a prison cell for a throne room. After correctly interpreting Pharaoh's dream, Joseph was made second commander over all of Egypt. What an honor. His dream had finally come true. Kinda.

Pharaoh told him, "Without your word no one will lift hand or foot in all of Egypt." Wow. In the words of the genie in the Disney movie *Aladdin*, "phenomenal cosmic powers"[1] were given to Joseph. Sounds incredible. What would he do with all this power? The following verses tell us how he would spend the next few years of his life. We learn "Joseph collected all the food produced in those seven years of abundance in Egypt and stored it in the cities." Wait a minute. He was made second-in-command over all of Egypt. He had all the power of a king. And yet, all his time was spent gathering food. After so many years of dreaming, I wonder if this is the work he had imagined. Maybe Joseph wanted to fight for prison reform after what he endured or perhaps use his freedom to escape the country that had enslaved him for so long. I think most people might have argued for a greater platform to use all that influence they had just been given. But any power he had was limited to the work that Pharaoh had given him to do.

There is another unfair advantage here that Joseph, as well as every leader, teacher, disciple, and Christian, must understand. We are limited. If given charge over a multitude of things, we would do poorly but if over only a few things, we could be so much more effective. We live in an age where everyone wants to do it all. The problem is that the person who tries to do everything is the person who ends up doing nothing. We were created to have limits, and success comes from being single-minded on one big task at a time. You cannot do everything, but you can do something.

Of all the chapter topics in this book, this one is my biggest weakness. I want to be good at everything. It's in my nature to try to focus on multiple things at a time. In any season of my life, if you were to ask me what I've been up to, I would be able to list five major objectives that I am trying to accomplish. I have always taken on more and more projects because I have lived by the slogan "I can do all things through . . . multitasking." Yikes! Can I be honest? It never works out well. As much as I hate to admit it, I am limited. I am not supposed to do everything. Only God can do that. I am only meant to do what God is calling me to at this very moment.

TIME TO FOCUS

In chapter 1 I shared a quote from Jim Elliot that has become my life motto: "Wherever you are, be all there." It is an anthem I continually recite to myself in this very distracting world. Let me tell you how I first heard it during my very first year in ministry. It was 2005 and I was serving as a missionary in Sri Lanka right after a tsunami ravaged the country. I was traveling around the island doing ministry projects with my friend Charlynn, who has served the Lord for years as a clown. She has brought smiles and hope to some of the poorest villages around the globe through her simple yet significant gospel presentations.

As Charlynn and I went to project after project, I became increasingly distracted. Katie and I were dating long-distance and every chance I could get, I would be thinking about her or trying to contact her. Wherever we were I would take out my phone, almost unaware of the ministry that was going on around me.

Finally Charlynn had enough of my divided attention. As we traveled to our next destination, she looked me straight in the eyes and asked, "Aaron, where are you?"

I responded with the obvious. "I am sitting in this van."

"No!" she exclaimed. "Where are you *really*?" And then she said the words that would change my life. "Aaron, wherever you are, be all there."

Joseph may have been given unlimited power, but he understood the unfair advantage of focusing only on what was in front of him. The famine was coming. It was not a time to work on anything else.

Lack of focus is a well-known problem in our society. Many books are being written on it. One of the best I have read is *Stolen Focus* by Johann Hari. In it, Hari writes that a small study showed students working on a computer would focus on something for an average of nineteen seconds.[2] Nineteen seconds! Holy cow. What are we thinking? The problem is that attention is a limited resource, and while it is going in multiple different directions, it is truly doing nothing important.

Light is a great example. With a single light bulb, I can illuminate a dark bedroom. Light has power. It touches every part of the room, but it makes no lasting impact on anything. A laser, on the other hand, is a light that can cut through steel. How can one light do nothing and another light do so much? The answer is focus. A laser is simply focused light. And sunlight may seem harmless, but you might be able to guess what happens if you give a magnifying glass to a ten-year-old boy on a sunny day. Just a little bit of focus on some poor ants on a sidewalk and *zap, zap, zap*. Focus always makes an impact. And concentration produces consequences.

Every person I know can be put into one of two categories: the chicken or the eagle. A chicken has zero focus. They eat whatever scraps are thrown on the ground right underneath them. You can put a steak on a counter and a chicken will never know, because chickens are too busy with all the trash thrown on the ground. An eagle is different. Eagles fly two miles above the earth. They are not focused on the trash on the ground; they are looking for the prized animal that can be their dinner. From two miles away, the eagle can spot the rabbit or mouse that will soon become its prey. This is where we get the expression "eagle eyes," because that eagle will focus all its attention on that one rodent.

What is the focus God has for your life right now? Part of thriving in your season is knowing what season God has you in. Pray about what you are called to and what your focus should be now. Make the goal clear because the distractions are numerous. If you don't have a distinct objective in focus, you will waste time getting nothing done. So remove your

> Remove your chicken tendencies and embrace the eagle approach.

chicken tendencies and embrace the eagle approach. It is hard, but it is doable.

Multitasking is a lie. The future belongs to those who learn to focus. Jesus was focused. His primary task was taking up the cross and offering his life as a sacrifice for our sins. This is why the Scriptures say, "As the time approached for him to be taken up to heaven, Jesus resolutely set out for Jerusalem" (Luke 9:51). That language is strong. Jesus was resolute about his priority. He could have done many things, but he focused on the main thing. Don't just do good things; do the God thing. What does God have for you to focus on?

The apostle Paul was also focused. He wrote, "Brothers and sisters, I do not consider myself yet to have taken hold of it. But one thing I do: Forgetting what is behind and straining toward what is ahead" (Phil. 3:13). How many things did Paul focus on? One! In the book of Acts, we see Paul being "compelled by the Spirit" to go to Jerusalem (Acts 20:22). Everyone was trying to talk him out of it, but Paul was focused on what God had for him. Pursuing a singular focus could be the unfair advantage that drives you to your ultimate purpose.

IDENTIFYING YOUR MOMENT

In a world that has so many options, how do we know what we should focus on? The apostle Paul gave us a strategy in

Ephesians 5 for removing distractions and embracing the moment God has us in:

> Be very careful, then, how you live—not as unwise but as wise, making the most of every opportunity, because the days are evil. Therefore do not be foolish, but understand what the Lord's will is. Do not get drunk on wine, which leads to debauchery. Instead, be filled with the Spirit. (vv. 15–18)

There are three practices seen within this passage that are helpful for each of us as we navigate how to handle our present moment. The first comes from the instruction to "be very careful, then, how you live . . . making the most of every opportunity" (Eph. 5:15–16). To make the most of our moments, we must be alert. We need to pay attention to our attention. This exercise is called *metacognition*, and it just means we need to be mindful of what we are thinking about.

Just the other day as I was driving home, I had this moment where metacognition kicked in and I realized, *I don't remember driving the last ten minutes*. I was so focused on the meeting I was going to that I zoned out, regardless of the fact I was driving a 5,700-pound SUV. Thank God my inattention didn't cause an accident. I can see now why Paul said, "Be very careful!" The problem is not that we aren't thinking. The issue is that we aren't thinking carefully. As we realize this, let's begin to carefully evaluate what we are giving our thoughts to. Am I staying focused as I read my Bible? Am I giving the person in front of me my best attention? Am I doing my work with excellence? Am I making the most of my date night, my kid's recital, or my friend's birthday? Pay attention to your attention.

Paul continued his challenge by saying, "Therefore do not be foolish, but understand what the Lord's will is" (Eph. 5:17). This is a nice way of saying, "Not everything you are doing is the Lord's will." So our second practice is to learn to say no to some good things so we can say yes to some God things. Let's be real: often we aren't all there because we are everywhere. Life can be far too busy, mostly because we do not know how to say no. This is honestly something I really wrestle with. I can struggle with being a people pleaser. I find a lot of validation in helping people and in being reliable. The problem is when I continually say yes to every good thing, I have no margin left when I encounter a God thing.

A few years into starting full-time ministry, I was completely overwhelmed, with no time or energy to manage the many different tasks and people I felt responsible for. In a state of exhaustion, I sat down with my pastor and told him how my busy lifestyle was affecting me. I showed him my packed schedule and my never-ending commitments, and I asked him for the secret of how to get all these amazing things done. He looked at me with his years of wisdom and kindly responded, "Well, Aaron, you are stressed because you are doing many of these things out of God's will." Excuse me?! That's offensive. What he said next, however, has stuck with me for over a decade. He said, "God has given you all the time that you need to do everything that he asks. So if you feel like you don't have enough time, it's because you are doing things he never asked you to do." Boom! I was instantly convicted by the truth in his words. As I once again looked over my overbooked calendar, I knew my pastor was right.

So how do you decide what things to say yes to? Picture with me a dartboard target. The bull's-eye is in the middle and every few inches out is another ring. I look at these as my priority circles. Those things closest to the center should get the greatest yes in my life. At the bull's-eye is my relationship with God. When I win spiritually, I win everywhere. God always gets my first yes.

For my life, the next priority circle that extends out from the middle belongs to my wife and kids. Sadly, it is sometimes those who should get most of our attention who receive the worst of us. I have been guilty of this many times, and these priority circles have helped me see that. After my family comes the priority of my calling. This is not my job. A job is how I make a living; a calling is how I experience true life. A job is about a paycheck; a calling is about a purpose. A job is about income; a calling is about impact. I'm not saying a job should ever be neglected, but when there is the power to choose, be careful what you are giving your yes to.

As the circles get farther out, so should your obligations to say yes. One Sunday I drew this illustration for my church and had the final circle say "everyone else." These are all the other people who have my attention outside of God, my family, and my ministry. I then asked the question "Where does social media put your attention?" The answer was obvious. Social media gives far too much attention to the circles that are not your priorities. Social media isn't bad, but if we are not careful it can begin to steal our attention from someone or something that should have that place of importance in our lives. As you consider your own priority circles, pay attention to what you are giving most of your yes to and evaluate if any changes need to be made.

The final practice we learn from the Ephesians passage comes from Paul's challenge, "Do not get drunk on wine, which leads to debauchery. Instead, be filled with the Spirit" (Eph. 5:18). What does getting drunk on wine do? It takes the edge off. It covers the pain. It numbs what is hurt and lets off some of the tension. Paul told us there is a better way: "Be filled with the Spirit." Release the pressure by relying on his presence.

The weight of the world bears down on all of us. As I write this, our society is shaken by a failing economy, a divisive election, a global pandemic, racial tensions, and so much more. These worldly burdens are intensified by pressures we face personally. Each of us carries countless roles that are vying for our attention: parent, spouse, friend, employee, coworker, leader, and child. Most significantly, we carry the role of a follower of Christ—a Christian.

The load can feel immense under the weight of so much responsibility. No wonder Paul realized our tendency to release the pressure by running to alcohol. Intoxication provides only counterfeit relief, however. There is only one true source of peace and direction. God's presence empowers us to make the most of the season we are in. Left on our own, we are only simple dreamers. But with God's power we are more than capable of accomplishing all he wants us to. You plus God equals a majority. God plus you equals a great parent, a great spouse, a great friend, a great entrepreneur. You can do so much, as long as you are not doing it alone. The same Spirit that raised Jesus from the dead is living inside of you. Your dreams are not too big, but they are impossible if you chase them without God.

Without God you will end up burned out and bummed out. Your own strength is limited, but our God is limitless. With his help, you can dream about the future and make an impact in the present. This is possible with God's power at work within you. Why don't you invite him in? Give him control. Before you move on to the next section, take a second and pray for God to fill you with his Spirit. Ask him to empower you to savor every moment in the present as you store in your heart the dream he has given you for the future.

To recap our three practices in being present:

1. Pay attention to your attention.
2. Learn to say no to good things so you can say yes to God things.
3. Release the pressure by relying on his presence.

THE ADVANTAGE OF ACTION

The difference between those who do something and those who don't do something is that those who do something *do* something. This is a simple but monumental concept in a world that values big dreams but does not love to start small. Earlier we considered how Joseph may have felt limited in his role. You, too, may be disappointed by the lack of opportunities you have been given. The reason for this can come in many forms: a dead-end job, a stifling family circumstance, a personal weakness, or a difficult leader. There are many reasons you may feel held back from what you would love to be doing.

When moments are most frustrating, this is where the unfair advantage comes in. When I can't do everything, I can choose to do something. These are the times to make the most of what is right in front of you, even if it appears smaller than you'd like. The best biblical teaching on this comes from the parable of the talents, a story told by Jesus himself.

Let me break it down.

> Again, it will be like a man going on a journey, who called his servants and entrusted his wealth to them. (Matt. 25:14)

God is the owner of all creation and all the creatures within it, and we are called to be his stewards. Everything belongs to him. Our time, our wealth (or lack of it), our environments, and our families are all under the authority and control of the Lord. So, big or small, every resource we have and every gift we have been given is from him.

Nothing is by accident. God has entrusted us with what's around us. We should wake up every day with an attitude of gratitude. Everything we have is a gift from God. There is nothing too small or insignificant when God is involved.

And look what happens.

To one he gave five bags of gold, to another two bags, and to another one bag, each according to his ability. Then he went on his journey. (v. 15)

Now, this is weird because it's so countercultural. In our culture we think everything should be fair. I hate to be the bearer of bad news, but opportunities in life aren't distributed fairly. This is why socialism doesn't work. If you took all the money in the world and divided it up equally, it wouldn't take long before most of it was back in the pockets of a select few, while others would find themselves in poverty.

Distributing everything evenly sounds like the perfect solution, but a pattern of failures throughout history has proven that it never works. A collapse in government is always the end result.

Let me give you another example.

I'll preface this by saying I don't drink Coke, and the first rule of giving up soda is to tell people about it every chance you get. But imagine you walk up to a Coke machine and on the front of the machine is a huge Out of Order sign. Now, who in their right mind would still try to put money in there? When a vending machine is out of order, it can't handle what you are putting into it. It's unproductive, unable to do what it was created to do.

I wonder how many people are walking around with a big Out of Order sign on their lives. For one reason or another, they are unable to complete the task that God has given them. They can't handle new assignments because they are not equipped to care for what they already have.

If you are frustrated by a lack of opportunities, take some

time to evaluate how you have been handling what is already in front of you. Instead of focusing on open doors, it might be wise to use this season to focus on personal development. As your abilities grow, opportunities will grow. To increase your ministry, focus on your current abilities. And always work at getting better.

God is a good owner, and he won't distribute more opportunities if you don't know how to handle them. The next part of the story says,

> The man who had received five bags of gold went at once and put his money to work and gained five bags more. So also, the one with two bags of gold gained two more. But the man who had received one bag went off, dug a hole in the ground and hid his master's money.
>
> After a long time the master of those servants returned and settled accounts with them. (vv. 16–19)

Just let me pause to make sure you read that correctly. Our master will return and settle accounts. Jesus is coming back. We will not be judged based on our good intentions, but on how faithful we have been to what God has entrusted us with. We are saved by grace, but the Bible is clear that we will be judged based on how we lived. Did we do what God wanted us to do with the life that he handed each of us?

> The man who had received five bags of gold brought the other five. "Master," he said, "you entrusted me with five bags of gold. See, I have gained five more." His master replied, "Well done, good and faithful servant! You have

been faithful with a few things; I will put you in charge of many things. Come and share your master's happiness!"

The man with two bags of gold also came. "Master," he said, "you entrusted me with two bags of gold; see, I have gained two more." His master replied, "Well done, good and faithful servant! You have been faithful with a few things; I will put you in charge of many things. Come and share your master's happiness!" (vv. 20–23)

These servants were faithful in what had been handed to them. They put the gifts to good use. And we see the advantage of their actions in how their gifts were multiplied. Our lesson in this: Don't just sit on your gift, activate it. Don't keep it hidden and don't waste what you have been given. Use it. Invest it. Put it into action. When we activate what God has given us, no matter how small, it develops us and opens up new opportunities. I am constantly asked by younger staff members for the opportunity to preach. What they don't realize is that I have already been watching how seriously they are stewarding a three-minute ministry moment or a ten-minute prayer devotional. If someone is not faithful in the small and if they are not investing in the little, then they are not ready to be given anything bigger.

So don't spend your life; invest it. Invest it in the small opportunities God has put in front of you. The first two servants in the parable worked well at what the owner had given them, and as a result, he gave them more. In your life, you have been given specific time, resources, and people. Steward them well. If you are a follower of Christ, you have also been entrusted with the Word of God and spiritual gifts

Stewardship paves a way for you to experience the blessing of God in your life.

given by the Holy Spirit. These are blessings that should always be activated to glorify God to the world around us. If you are praying for something more, remember what you have already been given. Be dedicated with what you have. We can trust that God is always faithful. You do your part, and watch God do his part. Stewardship paves a way for you to experience the blessing of God in your life.

If you are familiar with this parable, then you know that it ends super sad. The one who was given the smallest amount did nothing with it.

Then the man who had received one bag of gold came. "Master," he said, "I knew that you are a hard man, harvesting where you have not sown and gathering where you have not scattered seed. So I was afraid and went out and hid your gold in the ground. See, here is what belongs to you."

His master replied, "You wicked, lazy servant! So you knew that I harvest where I have not sown and gather where I have not scattered seed? Well then, you should have put my money on deposit with the bankers, so that when I returned I would have received it back with interest.

"So take the bag of gold from him and give it to the one who has ten bags. For whoever has will be given more, and they will have an abundance. Whoever does not have, even what they have will be taken from them. And throw that worthless servant outside, into the darkness, where there will be weeping and gnashing of teeth." (vv. 24–30)

This ending may sound harsh at first, but it is actually very just. The owner gave the servant his trust, and the servant was negligent with it. The servant was fearful rather than faithful to the owner who had always provided. And the servant was selfish by holding on to something that was not really his. By neglecting the owner's gift, not only was he not promoted, he also faced punishment. I know the pain of feeling like you have little to offer. But it is when you offer your little to God that multiplication happens. Remember the young boy with the five loaves and two fish? In his hands it was a Popeyes lunch. It could have fed him for probably a day. But handed over and activated in the hands of God, it fed five thousand with lots of leftovers. Your gift might seem small to you, but when you activate and start investing in it, you will see it grow into something supernatural. Dream for what is next, but don't forget to start now.

DIFFERENT, NOT DONE

As a result of Joseph's supernatural rise to power, he spent the next seven years gathering crops from around Egypt. In the dream he had as a teenager, he was in a place of prominence but his family was also with him. The promotion given by Pharaoh was certainly better than prison, but it was still not what he had been promised. This dream was different . . . but it was not done. When I planted our church, I had dreams I still have not seen fulfilled a decade into it. But one of the encouraging things God has spoken to me is that the dream may look different than I expected, but that doesn't mean it is done.

It is very easy to confuse "different" with "done." It is easy to assume because a dream did not happen in the way we wanted, God must be done with it. If you are in one of these seasons, let me encourage you. Just because it looks different doesn't mean it can't still be the dream God has for you. Different isn't bad, it is just . . . different. Each of us has had those moments of looking around and thinking things didn't turn out quite like we expected. This is normal! The marriage is different than you thought it would be. The kids turned out different than you thought. The business didn't grow like you thought. Your health didn't behave like you thought. The ministry didn't bear as much fruit as you thought. Things may look very different. But that doesn't mean they are done. We should be so careful that we don't confuse "different" as God's way of saying that he is done with us. Nothing could be further from the truth.

Joseph experienced "different," but God was far from done. New seasons and new positions are things God uses to expand us, not to expire us.

Elisabeth Elliot's story has always been inspiring. I heard her speak when I was in middle school, and her passion for purity and the gospel was contagious. She and her husband, Jim, met at Wheaton College where they both had a heart for reaching unreached tribes for Jesus. They married in

1953 in Ecuador, where they were both serving as missionaries. Soon after the birth of their daughter, Jim and four of his missionary companions began to make contact with a remote Huaorani tribe. This tribe was called the Aucas by their neighbors, which means *savages*. They had never heard the gospel, and the missionaries were passionate about telling them about Jesus. Sadly, though, on one contact into Huaorani territory, all five missionaries were unexpectedly and brutally speared to death.

The news of Jim's death made international newspapers. Elisabeth Elliot was now a widow and a single mother to their baby girl, Valerie. If anyone could imagine their season as being done, it would have been Elisabeth Elliot. The logical thing would have been to return to the States and raise her daughter in a safe environment. Her dream was done. But Elisabeth knew even though things now looked very different from what she had planned, it wasn't done. She continued to live among the people of Ecuador and for the next two years courageously worked on building a bridge of communication with the Huaorani tribe.

Elisabeth lived her life in total abandonment to whatever the Lord had for her. She said, "As long as this is what the Lord requires of me, then all else is irrelevant."[3] Her daughter was three years old when she took her greatest test of faith and moved in with the tribe that had murdered her husband.

The gospel, through the vessel of Elisabeth Elliot, changed the lives of that tribe. "The gospel they preached resulted in a marked decline in violence among tribe members, together with numerous conversions to Christianity and the growth of the local church."⁴ Elisabeth continued working in Ecuador until 1963 before moving back the United States. During this time, she wrote what is now a Christian classic, *Through Gates of Splendor.*

Elisabeth's life continued to be marked by "different." She married a professor from Gordon-Conwell Theological Seminary only to have him pass away less than four years after they married. This was the second husband who had died within a few years of getting married. Talk about tragedy. But Elisabeth never gave up. She eventually wrote over a dozen books, spoke around the globe, and even had a daily radio program. The circumstances of her life were always changing, but her calling never did.

Seasons change. Suffering happens. Loss, disappointment, and the unexpected are normal occurrences in our broken world. But even though our dreams may seem altered, nothing can destroy the plan of God. Things can be different, but that doesn't mean God is done. Different means deeper. Different means diversification. But different does not mean done.

God often takes us into unexpected seasons because there are different people we are called to reach. Joseph stewarded well each moment he was given, so God brought him into the palace to speak into the life of Pharaoh. In every season, there are people you are called to impact.

Like Joseph, the great missionary Paul also spent significant time in prison. One of those instances is mentioned in Acts 16. He was thrown into a cell with his friend Silas for preaching the gospel. As the two worshiped, the Lord sent an earthquake around midnight to open the cell doors and break off their chains. The jailer saw the doors opened and, believing every prisoner under his watch had escaped, took out his sword to kill himself.

Before he could, though, Paul and Silas stopped him. "Don't harm yourself! We are all here!" (Acts 16:28). The man ran to them and cried out, "What must I do to be saved?" (v. 30). This very different season created a moment for a different person than Paul and Silas planned for. As a result, the man and his entire household turned to Christ and were baptized. What if God knew the best way to reach this jailer was to put two of his best in the prison he was in charge of? The prison was the necessary place for this one person to be reached.

It might look different, but God is not done. Don't give up. Some of the best ministries happen after some of the biggest moments of pain. I love how Paul and Silas didn't complain about prison. They praised in the prison. And as they did so, the jailer found the Lord. Elisabeth didn't waste her life complaining about her loss. She fixed her eyes ahead and continued to reach more people for Jesus. Pain doesn't mean you are done. It just means that life looks different.

THE UNFAIR ADVANTAGE: STEWARD YOUR SEASON

When the famine eventually hit Egypt, Joseph's hard work made him a hero. The truth is that success isn't an overnight event. It is achieved only through daily diligence. It took Joseph years of faithfulness to accomplish what he was called to do. The beauty in Joseph's story is now we see that those seven years of gathering were just part of God's plan. All those years of abuse, slavery, and imprisonment led him to the moment when the entire region would be saved. What an amazing moment it must have been for Joseph to see the dream from so many years before finally become a reality. Each season he had been faithful with the little he had been given, and in return God brought him to where he was always meant to be.

What has been given to us is a gift from God; what we do with it is our gift back to him. He places opportunities in our lap. Some of the seasons may seem unfair. But these are the times when we best learn the value of stewardship and personal growth. These limited seasons are more of an advantage than we realize. Paul wrote that we are "servants of Christ and . . . entrusted with the mysteries God has revealed. Now it is required that those who have been given a trust must prove faithful" (1 Cor. 4:1–2). Whatever God has given is a big deal. Take care of it. How you handle this season determines a lot about the next.

If limitations have left you feeling disappointed and defeated, it can be so tempting to want to just give up. The unfair advantage, however, reminds you to keep sowing in this season, knowing that God will be faithful in this moment and the next. I have seen his faithfulness as I have navigated many different phases in my own life. Some of these times have been enjoyable, while others have been difficult. But as I have been intentional with whatever he has given, he has always been intentional in what he brought next. As I consistently followed him, he lovingly directed me to the next thing. I see how going on the mission field after college provided the next opportunity to become a youth pastor. And those six years with teenagers gave me the best preparation for when God called me to plant a church. And now, pastoring through the good seasons and the bad has continued to equip me for and open up more opportunities from God. He has always been faithful, and I will continue to be faithful to whatever he has given. We are far from perfect, of course. Even when we stumble and fail to follow his plan, he remains faithful and will redirect our steps as we return to him.

The truth is, if you embrace the moment God has you in, then God can do more in that moment than you can imagine. You can't do everything, but you can do exactly what God wants you to do right now. You can't please everyone, but you can please God. You might not change the world, but you can change someone's world. So stay focused. Stay faithful. And do whatever God has put in front of you right now. We can always be thankful, knowing it is often through our limitations God brings big things out of the little things. This is the unfair advantage.

> You can't do everything, but you can do exactly what God wants you to do right now.

DISCUSSION QUESTIONS

In this chapter we learned that we are limited. Our future is determined by our focus. I have found it necessary to have strategic moments of reflection throughout the year to make sure I am focusing on what I need to focus on. Here are four questions I ask that I invite you to think about as well:

1. What are the top priorities of your life during this season?
2. What measurable outcomes can you write down to evaluate your effectiveness over the next three months?
3. What "good" can you eliminate from your schedule that is keeping you from achieving something great?
4. In what ways does your calendar reflect your priorities? (How can you give your best goals your best time?)

DISCOVERING YOUR UNFAIR ADVANTAGE

One of the key missions God has given me is to help people walk into their ultimate God-ordained purpose. It is difficult to develop a calling you haven't discovered. I want to finish out this book with one of the most practical equations I have used for years to help people in this very area. You want to know your unfair advantage? Lean into this conclusion; it is the culmination of all the previous information in the book that was necessary to get you to this point.

Here is the equation that will change your life.

My personality + my passions + my pain = God's plan

I hope you can see the breakdown. Most gifts assessments will focus on your personality (design) and your passion (what wakes you up in the morning), but as we see throughout this book, our pain always plays a significant role in our purpose. Remember, nothing is wasted for God.

What is your personality like? There are so many personality tests and assessments out there—2,500 in the United States alone! I feel like I may have taken them all—DISC, Myers-Briggs, Enneagram, and so on. I am actually a big fan of whatever works for you. The key to them is to understand a little more about who God designed you to be. Your design is deliberate. You are unique on purpose. And when you are more self-aware, then you can become more purpose-aware. Understanding more about who you are also creates the opportunity to grow in areas where you are weak.

We often like to make excuses for our personality. We blame our bad tempers, our laziness, our lack of discipline, and our greed on it. We justify the bad with "That's just the way I am." But when we give our lives to Christ, this excuse no longer works. There may be weaknesses in us, but that is the result of a fallen world. After Christ, we should be on a daily quest of becoming like him. Instead of settling with our sinful flesh, we pray that God would redeem those parts of us and begin to make us holy. It may not happen overnight, but we can be committed every day to becoming better.

What are your passions? What are the things that excite you, that you love talking about and dreaming about? What keeps you up at night? Do you have a burden for something you just can't shake? It could be that the thing sparking the greatest drive in you is the thing God is speaking to you about. When I got the opportunity to go into the mission field, it was clear what my answer would be. A lifetime passion for travel, speaking, and sharing Jesus pointed me directly toward Sri Lanka. Ministry was so fun because I got to do what I had always loved doing.

There is a common strategy in churches to guilt people into serving on Sundays. I always found this to be counter-productive to the mission. We shouldn't serve based on guilt; we should do it based on gift. If it is something you are gifted in, usually it is something you are passionate about. I don't love golf, mostly because I am terrible at it. In the same way, I don't want people serving at the church who are there because they feel bad but because serving in that area makes them come alive.

There is a spiritual spin that can be put on every passion. If your passion is football, host a fantasy football league at your church and turn it into a small group. If your passion is food, practice hospitality. If your passion is listening, make yourself available. If your passion is your family, use that passion to lead them closer to Christ.

A lady in our church loves making jewelry. During the COVID-19 pandemic, we were raising money to care for people in our community who had lost their jobs. She decided to use her passion for jewelry to make a big difference. One day, she showed up to my office during the height of the crisis with a check for over $5,000—money earned from expressing her artistry through jewelry. She used her passion for a bigger purpose than herself. Your passion is part of your purpose.

In the equation of discovering your calling, the last part is to understand your pain. That is what this book has been about. We have identified seven painful seasons. You have probably lived through a few of them, if not all. There is an advantage to every unfair part of your story. As we have seen throughout this book, the story of Joseph's life was unfair. From being a solo dreamer, to facing rejection, to being overworked and underpaid, to guarding his integrity, to refusing to quit, Joseph's journey was far from an overnight success. His life was difficult, but it was for a purpose much bigger than he could have imagined.

Here are seven questions to ask yourself as you complete this book, followed by a few thoughts to help you reflect on each question.

1. What dream from God have you stopped dreaming?
2. How are you dealing with rejection?
3. Despite your pay, how is your work ethic?
4. Are you maintaining your integrity?
5. What opportunities are you embracing during this season?
6. How are you staying encouraged not to quit?
7. What is God trying to get you to focus on?

What dream from God have you stopped dreaming? Can I encourage you? Dream again. Get away if you need to. Take a weekend in the mountains. Go on a long walk. Enjoy a day at the beach. Find a space where you can get alone with God and begin to dream. Can you imagine being one of those stories that truly experiences breakthrough after a season of tragic failure?

The main point is to take a moment and really evaluate, "Why did I settle?"

Our God is too big, his purposes too great, and his power too real for us to settle for anything less than his ultimate best for our lives. If you gave up on a dream that he gave you, pick it back up today. Watch how this could be your unfair advantage.

How are you dealing with rejection? We all have experienced it. In 1993 there was unrest in Somalia, and the US Army's Delta Force was sent to grab a drug lord. Their Black Hawk helicopter was shot down and multiple soldiers were killed. In a horrible display, the bodies were dragged through the streets while the opposing army celebrated. The US government sent in a team to recover the bodies and any men who might have survived. If you have seen the movie *Black Hawk Down*, it recounts this story in gripping detail. The rescue team underwent major fire from every direction. As they tried to rescue different wounded soldiers, they realized how outnumbered they were. The colonel in charge stopped the vehicle, took in some wounded, and shouted at a bleeding sergeant standing in shock nearby:

Colonel: Get into that truck and drive.
Sergeant: But I'm shot, Colonel.
Colonel: Everybody's shot, get in and drive.[1]

It's a powerful message for all of us. We have all been shot. We have all been offended. We have all been rejected. It's time to move past the hurt. There have been major wounds, but it's time to let them heal. Instead of looking behind, drive toward the destination God has for your life. The Enemy wants to get you focused on the pain instead of your purpose. It is not about the rejection. Instead of allowing the words and actions of others to defeat you, allow God to use even this to propel you forward.

Get in the truck and drive.

Despite your pay, how is your work ethic? Maybe you are going through a season where you feel overworked and underpaid. During my time as a youth pastor, I often felt like this. Youth ministry can feel like a 24/7 job. It's a lot of hours, a lot of energy, and a *lot* of emotions. And over those six years I received one raise of 5 percent. It was tough. It would have been easy to complain, but now I see the value in this difficult season.

If you are in similar circumstances, learn to embrace the discipline of working as unto the Lord (Col. 3:23). Instead of trying to get famous, why don't you lean into getting faithful? Take the season that you are in to be diligent with what God has given you to do. Our God is a great rewarder. He sees what you are doing in secret, so don't quit now. If you give it enough time, you will reap the benefits of your labor.

Are you maintaining your integrity? It is in times of intense temptation that our true character is shown. Follow the example of Joseph and flee the moments of temptation. When you do what no one else will do, you will reap the benefits everyone wants to reap. Purity promotes. When you fight for purity in your sexuality, your finances, your work, your word, and your life, you will experience such joy on the other side. If you feel like you have a larger-than-normal target on your life, it is not because the Enemy is angry about your past, but because the Enemy is threatened by your future. It can feel painful to stay pure, especially in a world that shames the godly and promotes the promiscuous. Don't give up or give in.

During my final service as a youth pastor many years ago, I stood at the side of the room during worship and watched hundreds of students I had invested years of my life in. I was so grateful for the time God allowed me with them. It is not lost on me how easy it would have been to lose my job, lose my influence, and lose my reputation if I had fallen to temptation during those years. Temptations will always be there. But the pain of staying pure is always worth it. Remember the *acharit*. The end result is worth maintaining your purity. You might not see the fruit here, but you have all of eternity to celebrate.

What opportunities are you embracing during this season? Prison is a dark place that could easily end in frustration. Joseph, however, used prison to help shape his future. The most beautiful pictures are usually developed in dark places. Our church has seen this over the last decade. We launched in a small theater in the middle of the community. As much as the theater has been a blessing, we have had problems with it since day one. Fire codes, lack of space, lease dilemmas, and issues with parking have been a constant plague to us.

Every time we have faced one of these obstacles, there

honestly never seems like a good solution. We feel the weight of needing a location, along with the burden of being stuck and not knowing how to make it work. We have had weeks where we didn't know if we would be able to open the doors on Sunday. It can seem almost hopeless. In these moments, we could have just accepted the situations and given up. But instead, we have learned to embrace the pain and get creative. We get to work, and as we do, God gives us an answer to our obstacle. Over the years, there have been countless times we have been in this stuck situation, and as we kept praying and kept working, God has always provided a supernatural answer for us. Every single time.

The most creative ideas are usually launched out of a season of lack. When we have little, he multiplies it. Through the dark seasons we are able to discover those bigger opportunities.

How are you staying encouraged not to quit? Maybe you are growing discouraged by how long something is taking. Don't throw in the towel. Stay persistent as you work toward whatever dream God has planted in you. You have no clue how close you are to a breakthrough. If the dream God put in your heart is not in its mature state, maybe it is because you are not either. Take some time and recommit to the hidden season of preparation. This could be your ultimate unfair advantage. You will win if you simply don't quit. Most people who are considered successful aren't really that gifted; they just have more grit to keep going when everyone else quits. Have that kind of tenacity and watch how God will honor it. I am just starting to reap benefits in my late thirties that I dreamed about in my teenage years. One reason is I didn't quit when everyone else threw in the towel.

Last, **what is God trying to get you to focus on?** Remember my life motto, "Wherever you are, be all there." Stay focused on your assignment, whatever it is—big or small. You can't do everything, but you can do something. Missionary David Livingstone is quoted as saying, "Sympathy is no substitute for action." If you can't preach to the masses, preach to the one (or to the eleven). If you can't give millions of dollars, give what you can. If you can't solve the global adoption problem, solve it for one kid's life. Do for one what you wish you could do for everyone. It's painful to start small and stay focused, but it is part of the pain that leads you to your purpose.

These seven questions sum up the book. Every season is painful. But it is pain that will help lead you to God's plan. It takes more than personality and passion to figure out your calling. It also takes pain, and that is the unfair advantage. When handled well, the rough times shape us and take us the farthest.

FINAL THOUGHTS ON PAIN

Pain, by itself, does not lead to the advantages we have been discussing. When left unchecked, pain can cause damage to ourselves and others. It is not enough to recognize the hurt; you also have to respond to it in a God-honoring way. My prayer is that you would take some time and commit to God that you will embrace that unfair situation God's way instead of man's way. God is clear that "my ways [are] higher than your ways and my thoughts than your thoughts" (Isa. 55:9). When confronted by an unfair situation, you have a choice to make: God's way or man's way? Man's way "seems right to a man, but its end is the way of death" (Prov. 14:12 NKJV).

Man's way of dealing with a failed dream = settle for less
God's way of dealing with a failed dream = keep dreaming

Man's way of dealing with rejection = get offended
God's way of dealing with rejection = use it for redirection

Man's way of dealing with being underpaid = slack off
God's way of dealing with being underpaid = work harder

Man's way of dealing with temptation = whatever feels good, do it
God's way of dealing with temptation = maintain your integrity

Man's way of being in a difficult season = whine
God's way of being in a difficult season = work

Man's way of dealing with being forgotten = throw in the towel

God's way of dealing with being forgotten = don't
quit, and trust God's timing

Man's way of having limited opportunities = get
entitled
God's way of dealing with limited opportunities = get
focused

One day you will look back and see how the difficult seasons were crucial in getting you to where God was calling you. Life is not about what happens to you; it is about how you handle what happens to you. Will you embrace it God's way or man's way? The choice is yours.

There is an advantage we have not yet discussed, but it is a significant one. Going through pain qualifies you to give help and compassion to people you would not have been able to otherwise. Our struggles are not meant merely to be learned from. They are to be leveraged for the greater good. People need to hear about what you have gone through in a way that helps and encourages them through their own difficulties. In our social media culture, we are too focused on impressing people with our strengths instead of impacting people with our struggles.

Your story becomes a sermon when it is shared with people to give them hope. If you have gone through something, there is purpose in it. And that purpose can really benefit someone who is going through something similar. Think of Joseph. Countless lives were transformed because of what he endured.

Your story has significance if it is shared. When you

share how God used your pain, it gives people purpose in what they are going through. It helps them know there is a reason behind this rough season. Remembering what God has done in the past gives people hope for what he can do in the future. If God did it for you, he will do it for someone else.

I would take it a step further and say it is selfish not to share how your pain ended up being for a greater purpose. Your testimony should reveal some of your test. Your ministry should highlight your misery. We are human beings who have suffered, and no one wants to learn from perfect people, outside of Jesus. We need what you have gone through. Do you have an outlet to share it? Two women who go to my church had abortions years ago when they were in their early twenties. They each have suffered under the weight of that decision, spending many years in pain over it. One day, birthed out of a compassion only they would understand, they decided to start a small group to help others who were also battling this life-altering decision. The group has created a space for women to heal, and it would never have been available if these women hadn't allowed their pain to help them see who else was hurting. It is allowing God to turn the bad into something good.

> Your testimony should reveal some of your test.

You might impress people with your strengths, but you impact them with your struggles. If it happened to you, let it help people after you. The path might have looked unfair, but eventually the platform will seem unfair. Don't let people judge your stage when they don't know your struggle. They will think you are an overnight success. You know the truth. You embraced the unfair and used it for a greater advantage. We often go through what no one else is going through to get to a place of impact very few ever reach. I look forward to seeing how God uses your life, your pain, and your heartache to bring you to positions that truly change the world.

We live life forward, but we understand life backward. The only way to truly embrace hard seasons is to know these seasons are frustrating but also foundational. Our lives might look strange, but our God is very strategic. When you look backward you will see how every difficult moment was developmental for where God was taking you.

Vision to keep going gives pain purpose. When you know there is an ultimate calling for your life, you can embrace the pain to help you get there. The key is not to be driven by comfort but to be driven by calling.

Joseph kept his face forward through all the unfairness and all the pain. And his story didn't end with him staying alone in Egypt. The famine he predicted eventually took place. It affected a widespread area, and Joseph created a system where the known world would come to Egypt to buy grain. Guess who eventually came for help? Joseph's brothers. The very ones who tried to kill him would eventually beg him for food.

Joseph, now one of the most powerful men in the world, could have taken revenge and instantly had his brothers killed. But you don't feel your way through life; you *faith* your way through. So he didn't avenge himself. He looked at his brothers and said, "You intended to harm me, but God intended it for good to accomplish what is now being done, the saving of many lives" (Gen. 50:20).

If it hurts now, it will be helpful later.

It was clear those many years of pain had been for a purpose and his God was big enough to avenge him. Paul wrote, "Do not take revenge, my dear friends, but leave room for God's wrath, for it is written: 'It is mine to avenge; I will repay,' says the Lord" (Rom. 12:19).

Nothing is random with God. If it hurts now, it will be helpful later. In other words, he knew the bigger picture. Do you?

THINK LONG

I have to give one final caution as I close out this book. Our God does not operate on our timeline. Joseph's story neatly described the positive outcomes to seven painful moments. But that is not always the case for us. Many of our greatest successes will not be recognized on this side of eternity.

Here is a good reminder: life is short, but eternity is long. Our prayers work, but you might not see the fruit until you get to heaven. Our purity matters, but you might not see the reward until you stand before God. I wish that everyone who was mistreated for their faith could enjoy a final chapter where they become second-in-command over their nation. Usually that is not the case.

The fact is that your unfair advantage is not about earthly success. It truly is about the heavenly reward. My goal is not that man says, "Good job," but that God says, "Well done." If your goal is success in the eyes of men, you will never live fulfilled. This world is draining. But it is also not our home and not our prize. Heaven is.

Having kept that prize clearly in focus, Paul could proclaim near the end of his life, "I have fought the good fight, I have finished the race, I have kept the faith. Now there is in store for me the crown of righteousness, which the Lord, the righteous Judge, will award to me on that day—and not only to me, but also to all who have longed for his appearing" (2 Tim. 4:7–8). Our lifelong goal and our ultimate calling is obedience to God. This is what we work toward and what we fight for even during the worst moments and the darkest days. This is what will be rewarded in heaven. We embrace our pain now for the prize that is to come.

I hope you see a glimpse of the fruit on this planet, but remember that fruit takes time. Life on this side is short. Plant seeds now. There is a heavenly crown that is better than the recognition given to any earthly dignitary. Live in such a way that the fruit of your suffering will far outlast the moments of your life.

I will leave you with the words of the great missionary C. T. Studd, who ended up giving his life for the gospel: "Only one life, 'twill soon be past, Only what's done for Christ will last."[2] Keep plowing. Keep staying faithful. Keep embracing the pain of this earth. It's unfair, but it is for your advantage.

ACKNOWLEDGMENTS

This book is the result of numerous voices and influences in my life. First, I want to start with my parents, Riley and Susan. You raised me and my siblings right. We were taught to love God and use our lives to glorify Him. I'm grateful for both of you. Mom, I'm also grateful for the gift you gave me in writing.

Grandma, you taught me to pursue education and constantly learn.

Pastor Evon, thank you for giving me my first job in ministry. You believed in me and trained me when no one else would. I'm forever indebted to you.

Pastor Richard, you inspire me to be more like Christ, and I'm grateful for you.

Mark Batterson, you're the one who told me to write this book and that one word of encouragement changed my entire life.

My five children—Lily, Annabelle, Kai, Elise, and Adeline—I love you all with all my heart. I choose to live a life that you're proud of. You're all world changers.

Radiant Church, thank you for allowing me to live God's dream for my life. You're the kindest and most generous church, and I plan on pastoring you for decades to come.

Lastly, but most importantly, I'm grateful for Jesus. Without you, I'm nothing. With you, I can do all things. I love you.

NOTES

INTRODUCTION

1. Siobhán O'Grady, "The Coronavirus Intensified a Hunger Crisis Last Year, but 2021 Could Be Worse," *Washington Post*, January 6, 2021, https://www.washingtonpost.com/world/2021 /01/06/coronavirus-starvation-poverty-inequality-hunger-un/.
2. Fred Goodall, "Tom Brady Signs with the Tampa Bay Buccaneers," *The Florida Times-Union*, updated February 7, 2021, https://www.jacksonville.com/story/sports/nfl/2020/03/20 /tom-brady-signs-with-tampa-bay-buccaneers/112251556/.
3. Molly Kinder and Laura Stateler, "Amazon and Walmart Have Raked in Billions in Additional Profits During the Pandemic, and Shared Almost None of It with Their Workers," Brookings, December 22, 2020, https://www.brookings.edu/blog/the-avenue /2020/12/22/amazon-and-walmart-have-raked-in-billions-in -additional-profits-during-the-pandemic-and-shared-almost -none-of-it-with-their-workers/.
4. Steve Jobs, *The Pixar Story: A Documentary by Leslie Iwerks* (Burbank, CA: Disney Company, 2007), https://www .disneyplus.com/movies/the-pixar-story/.
5. Frank Lewis Dyer and Thomas Commerford Martin, *Edison: His Life and Inventions*, vol. 2 (New York: Harper & Brothers

Publishers, 1910), 616, https://books.google.com/books?id
=B7A4AAAAMAAJ&pg=PA616.

6. Concept from Danish philosopher Søren Kierkegaard. Howard
V. Hong and Edna H. Hong, trans. and eds., *Søren Kierkegaard's
Journals and Papers*, vol. 1 (Bloomington: Indiana University
Press, 1967), 450.

UNFAIR ADVANTAGE #1: THE DISCOURAGED DREAMER

1. Adam Hartung, "Listen to Competitors, Not Customers,"
Forbes, January 6, 2010, https://www.forbes.com/2010/01/06
/innovation-customers-competitors-leadership-managing
-marketing.html.

2. "24 People Who Became Highly Successful After Age 40,"
Business Insider: India, August 20, 2017, https://www
.businessinsider.in/retail/24-people-who-became-highly
-successful-after-age-40/slidelist/47789493.cms.

3. Drew Hansen, "Why Richard Branson and I Always Carry a
Notebook," *Forbes*, August 15, 2011, https://www.forbes.com
/sites/drewhansen/2011/08/15/why-richard-branson-and-i
-always-carry-a-notepad/.

4. Gregory Ciotti, "The Psychological Benefits of Writing:
Why Richard Branson and Warren Buffett Write Regularly,"
Entrepreneur, June 18, 2014, https://www.entrepreneur.com
/living/the-psychological-benefits-of-writing-why-richard
-branson/234712.

5. Kevin Kruse, "Richard Branson's Single Most Important Tool,"
Leadx, February 9, 2017, https://leadx.org/articles/richard
-bransons-single-important-tool/.

6. T. E. Lawrence, *Seven Pillars of Wisdom*, unabridged ed. (Garden
City, NY: Doubleday, Doran & Co., 1935).

7. Elisabeth Elliot, *Through Gates of Splendor* (1957; repr., Carol
Stream, IL: Tyndale, 2015), 20.

8. Motley Fool Staff, "Why George Bernard Shaw Wanted to Be
'Used,'" The Motley Fool, updated June 18, 2019, https://www
.fool.com/investing/2019/06/18/why-george-bernard-shaw
-wanted-to-be-used.aspx.

9. William Carey, "Expect Great Things; Attempt Great Things," Center for Study of the Life and Work of William Carey, updated April 7, 2014, https://www.wmcarey.edu/carey /expect/.

10. H. Jackson Brown, *P.S. I Love You* (Nashville: Rutledge Hill Press, 1990), 13.

UNFAIR ADVANTAGE #2: THE REDIRECTED REJECT

1. "What Is the Ratio of People to Sheep in New Zealand?," CulturalWorld, accessed April 17, 2023, https://www .culturalworld.org/what-is-the-ratio-of-people-to-sheep-in-new -zealand.htm.

2. Rachel Gillett, "How Walt Disney, Oprah Winfrey, and 19 Other Successful People Rebounded After Getting Fired," *Inc.*, October 6, 2015, https://www.inc.com/business-insider /21-successful-people-who-rebounded-after-getting-fired.html.

3. Gillett, "How Walt Disney, Oprah Winfrey, and 19 Other Successful People Rebounded."

4. "Thomas Edison," Biography, April 7, 2017, https://www .biography.com/inventor/thomas-edison#early-career.

5. Sarah Gamard, "Joe Biden Has Run for President Twice Before. Here's What Those Elections Looked Like," Delaware Online, updated April 26, 2019, https://www.delawareonline.com/story /news/politics/2019/04/25/how-joe-biden-ran-for-president-the -first-two-times/3571822002/.

6. Eric Zorn, "Without Failure, Jordan Would Be False Idol," *Chicago Tribune*, May 19, 1997, https://www.chicagotribune.com/news /ct-xpm-1997-05-19-9705190096-story.html.

7. Guy Winch, "10 Surprising Facts About Rejection," *Psychology Today*, July 3, 2013, item 1, https://www.psychologytoday.com /us/blog/the-squeaky-wheel/201307/10-surprising-facts -about-rejection.

8. Winch, "10 Surprising Facts About Rejection," item 6.

9. C. Truman Davis, "The Crucifixion of Jesus: The Passion of Christ from a Medical Point of View," in *Arizona Medicine* (March 1965), 183–87, quoted in Caleb Wilde, "Did Jesus Die of

a Broken Heart?," April 6, 2012, https://www.calebwilde.com /2012/04/did-jesus-die-of-a-broken-heart/.

10. Stefano Carnazzi, "Kintsugi: The Art of Precious Scars," Lifegate, January 30, 2016, https://www.lifegate.com/kintsugi.

UNFAIR ADVANTAGE #3: THE WAGELESS WORKER

1. Avery Hartmans, "Jeff Bezos Originally Wanted to Name Amazon 'Cadabra,' and 14 Other Little-Known Facts About the Early Days of the E-commerce Giant," *Business Insider*, July 2, 2021, https://www.businessinsider.com/jeff-bezos-amazon-history-facts -2017–4#amazon-got-started-out-of-bezos-garage-in-the-early -days-bezos-held-meetings-at-barnes-and-noble-4.

2. Max Nisen, "16 People Who Worked Incredibly Hard to Succeed," *Business Insider*, September 5, 2012, https://www.businessinsider .com/16-people-who-worked-incredibly-hard-to-succeed -2012–9.

3. Nisen, "16 People."

4. Corrie ten Boom, *Messages of God's Abundance* (Grand Rapids: Zondervan, 2002), 96.

5. John Maxwell, "Minute with Maxwell: Earning Trust," Maxwell Leadership, January 5, 2020, YouTube video, 4:37, https://www .youtube.com/watch?v=YsoCBquLGKg.

UNFAIR ADVANTAGE #4: THE SEDUCED SAINT

1. "Strong's Hebrew: 319. acharith," Bible Hub, accessed January 10, 2023, https://biblehub.com/hebrew/319.htm.

2. Kate Shellnutt, "Here's How America Is Praising Its Best-Known Preacher: Billy Graham," *Christianity Today*, February 21, 2018, https://www.christianitytoday.com/news/2018/february/how -america-is-praising-evangelist-billy-graham-tribute.html.

3. "Teens More Likely to Smoke if Parents Were Smokers, Even if They Quit Long Ago," Partnership to End Addiction, August 2013, https://drugfree.org/drug-and-alcohol-news /teens-more-likely-to-smoke-if-parents-were-smokers-even-if -they-quit-long-ago/.

4. John Maxwell, *Developing the Leader Within You* (Nashville: Thomas Nelson, 1993), 38, emphasis original.

5. Robert L. Jackson, "Ministry Makes $150 Million a Year: Rich Life Style Reflects Swaggart Empire Wealth," *Los Angeles Times*, March 14, 1988, https://www.latimes.com/archives/la-xpm-1988-03-14-mn-715-story.html; "$150 in 1987," CPI Inflation Calculator, accessed January 10, 2023, https://www.in2013dollars.com/us/inflation/1987?amount=150.

6. "The Origin of 'Hypocrite,'" Word History, *Merriam-Webster*, accessed January 10, 2023, https://www.merriam-webster.com/words-at-play/hypocrite-meaning-origin.

7. "Hunger 'Can Lead to Poor Decisions,' Dundee University Study Finds," BBC News, September 16, 2019, https://www.bbc.com/news/uk-scotland-tayside-central-49714239.

8. "Hunger 'Can Lead to Poor Decisions,'" BBC News.

9. Julie Dawn Cole, *Willy Wonka and the Chocolate Factory*, directed by Mel Stuart, screenplay by Roald Dahl (Hollywood: Paramount Pictures, 1971).

10. Patrick Lencioni, *The Ideal Team Player: How to Recognize and Cultivate the Three Essential Virtues* (San Francisco: Jossey-Bass, 2016).

11. Billy Graham, *Newsweek*, August 24, 1987, 11, quoted in John Maxwell, *Developing the Leader Within You* (Nashville: Thomas Nelson, 1993), 45.

UNFAIR ADVANTAGE #5: THE OPPRESSED OPPORTUNIST

1. John Bunyan, *Grace Abounding to the Chief of Sinners* (1666; repr., London: Religious Tract Society, 1905), para. 328, archived on Project Gutenberg, released February 19, 2013, https://www.gutenberg.org/files/654/654-h/654-h.htm.

2. Ali Abu Dashish, "Interested in Knowing More About Prisons in Ancient Egypt?," Sada Elbalad English, December 18, 2018, https://see.news/interested-in-knowing-more-about-prisons-in-ancient-egypt/.

3. Dashish, "Interested in Knowing More About Prisons in Ancient Egypt?"
4. Edgar Watson Howe, *Country Town Sayings* (Topeka: Crane & Co., 1911), 109, https://www.google.com/books/edition /Country_Town_Sayings/6KAfAQAAMAAJ.
5. Dale Carnegie, quoted in John Maxwell, *How to Influence People* (Nashville: HarperCollins Leadership, 2013), 62.

UNFAIR ADVANTAGE #6: THE FORGOTTEN FAITHFUL

1. Shrutika Srivastava, "How Much Pressure to Make a Diamond?," The Diamond Authority, accessed January 10, 2023, https://www.thediamondauthority.org/how-much-pressure -to-make-a-diamond/.
2. Cate Lineberry, "Diamonds Unearthed," *Smithsonian Magazine*, December 2006, https://www.smithsonianmag.com /science-nature/diamonds-unearthed-141629226/.
3. C. S. Lewis, *The Great Divorce*, (1946; repr., New York: HarperOne, 2001), 75, emphasis original.
4. "Giant Sequoia Questions," Giant Sequoia Nursery, accessed January 10, 2023, https://www.giant-sequoia.com/faqs/giant -sequoia-questions/.
5. Brian Krans, "Quitting Smoking? Expect a Lot of Failure Before You Succeed," Healthline, July 12, 2016, https://www .healthline.com/health-news/quitting-smoking-expect-failure -before-you-succeed.
6. Lauren Perkins, "Speaker Showcase: Michael Phelps," Champions: Olympic Speakers, August 26, 2021, https://olympic-speakers .com/news/speaker-showcase-michael-phelps.

UNFAIR ADVANTAGE #7: THE LIMITED LEADER

1. Robin Williams, *Aladdin*, directed by John Musker and Ron Clements (Burbank, CA: Walt Disney Company, 1992).
2. Johann Hari, *Stolen Focus: Why You Can't Pay Attention—And How to Think Deeply Again* (New York: Crown, 2022), 10.
3. Dave Littlewood, "Elisabeth Elliot: The Missionary Who Lived with the Tribe That Killed Her Husband," New Life Publishing,

March 5, 2022, https://www.newlifepublishing.co.uk/articles
/faith/elisabeth-elliot-the-missionary-who-lived-with-the-tribe
-that-killed-her-husband/.
4. Littlewood, "Elisabeth Elliot."

CONCLUSION

1. *Black Hawk Down*, directed by Ridley Scott (Santa Monica, CA:
   Jerry Bruckheimer Films, 2001).
2. From the poem "Only One Life" by C. T. Studd, archived on
   "Poetry About Jesus and Salvation," accessed January 10, 2023,
   http://cavaliersonly.com/poetry_by_christian_poets_of_the_past
   /only_one_life_twill_soon_be_past_-_poem_by_ct_studd.

ABOUT THE AUTHOR

Aaron Burke (DMin, MBA) is the lead pastor of Radiant Church, which he and his wife, Katie, started in 2013 after selling everything and moving in faith to a new city. Radiant Church now has eight campuses throughout the Tampa Bay community. Aaron's passions are building the local church and helping Christians live into their God-given potential. In addition to pastoring at Radiant, Aaron regularly speaks at churches and conferences across America. He also works heavily with planting churches and developing leaders in South Asia (Sri Lanka and India). His work with equipping leaders includes his *Made for More* leadership podcast and partnering with the Association of Related Churches (ARC) and the Church Multiplication Network (CMN) to train church planters. Aaron and his wife have been married since 2010 and have five beautiful children. He loves to travel, spend time with his family, and do CrossFit.